THAT'S
LIFE!
at least my version of it

THAT'S LIFE!

at least my version of it

PATRICIA K. WYMAN, PH.D.

Charleston, SC
www.PalmettoPublishing.com

That's Life! At Least My Version of It

Copyright © 2022 by Patricia K. Wyman, Ph.D.

First Edition

Hardcover ISBN: 979-8-88590-671-5
Paperback ISBN: 979-8-88590-672-2

Dedication

This book is for the rainbows of my life—my children, Lyndie and G.J., as well as my loving grandchildren: Owen, Tegan, Cole, Emery, Dane, Cade, Rocco, and Eli. Thank you for helping me to break the dysfunctional family cycle. It is also for My Honey, Steven, who gave me a second chance at getting love right. And lastly, I dedicate this book to teachers, all around the world, who have an opportunity to impact a child's life, even more than they might realize.

Contents

Acknowledgments

I would like to thank my friend, Shane Gureck, for his assistance with this project. Shane was able to gently push me to write a better book. The comments from his hard work and diligence, as my primary reader, made me realize that my book could impact a much larger audience than I had intended. Through his eyes, I could clearly see that I had a story worth telling.

A special shout out to the founder of "LIVE A GREAT STORY" who gave me permission to use their logo on a sweatshirt for my cover photograph. Check out Liveagreatstory.com to view their awesome products.

Cover photo credit goes to Steven P. Welch.

Sincere kudos to Savannah, Christina, Roy, and the rest of the Palmetto Publishing staff for their expertise, patience and painless guidance through this amazing writing process.

Foreword

By Shane Gureck

When I was a child, my mother took on a side-job cleaning houses as a means to support my brother and me. On one occasion, as a sort of "teaching moment," she told us about one of her clients who had recently displayed incredible compassion and generosity. This client, she told us, had repeatedly witnessed one of her neighbors struggling to enter and exit her car. The driver's side door handle was missing so the senior woman had to climb in through the passenger side every time she went anywhere. Unbeknownst to this person, the client hired a mechanic to fix the problem. I recall being slightly confused as to why somebody would carry out such a noble act without claiming credit, but the profoundness of the gesture has stayed with me ever since. This was the first life lesson that I learned from Dr. Patricia Wyman.

As time went on, she and my mother became friends and I would have the pleasure of getting to know her a little bit, here and there. Not long ago, I learned that Patty, as she was always known to us, had written a story about her life, and was seeking an uninvolved, impartial reader to look it over for her. Being an English minor and avid reader, I gladly accepted the task. Upon getting started, it didn't take long to realize that Patty's earlier display of integrity, which had resonated with me for so long, was merely one among the many impactful pieces of wisdom that she has to offer, to both myself, and the world.

While studying psychology at OSU, I was frequently taught that an individual's childhood and early life experiences are strong predictors of the person they will inevitably become. Children of divorce, for example, are twice as likely to drop out of high school, while 70% of prison inmates come from broken homes. These statistics are so prevalent and evident in life, that many of us tend to feel bound to our fate, helpless victims of our own circumstances. By recounting her life story, the writer masterfully demonstrates how she was able to overcome the adverse nature of her childhood and avoid becoming one of these dreaded statistics. Her story radiates inspiration; reminding us that there is plenty of good in life to be found, and that while some are graced from birth, many others are put to the test, and must proactively embark on a journey to find it.

In Patty's case, this journey starts at a very young age, and as her narrative begins to unfold, you are introduced to the instability and capriciousness that marked her childhood. You learn of the atrocities that she faced, many of which were brought about by her own family. The writer spends minimal time describing these particular events, supplying only the pertinent details, before quickly shifting focus back to the good times—the ones more in line with the vivacious, youthful, and lighthearted tone seen previously throughout the story. This uplifting tone mirrors her real-life personality and positive approach to life. Soon, it becomes abundantly clear that Patty is not one to ruminate or dwell on anything adverse or negative, which is perhaps the key foundation to her resiliency.

In addition to tone, the feeling of lighthearted wholesomeness which characterizes the story, is largely achieved through setting. Patty paints a beautiful picture of 1950s and 60s Cleveland, to invoke a sort of "old-fashioned" childhood nostalgia in the reader. As a thirty-year-old who never experienced these times, I found myself relating to, even yearning for, the simple joys produced from a scrap-yard game of baseball, and the mischievous thrills of pulling the fire alarm, or hearing the gasps of anticipation as you slowly inch your tongue closer to the frozen steel pole.

Patty's life is packed full of memorable childhood anecdotes involving activities like these, never falling short on humor and *"You kids are up to no good!"* moments. As Patty ages in the narrative, these anecdotes evolve into more adult-oriented topics like college, travel, and parenthood, yet still maintain the lighthearted and playful nature that is found in youth. This may suggest that the negative external factors that surrounded her as a child, were ultimately unable to change her positive attitude and outlook on life.

Through a stream-of-consciousness style of recollection, the writer essentially invites you into her mind as she revisits the memories of her past, welcoming you as an inside observer, rather than an outside one. This provides an intensely intimate and authentic experience. Often times you will come across non-sequiturs and emphasis on random, insignificant details when an event is being described. Our brain works in a similar non-linear fashion during the process of recollection, and this commonality elicits a closeness and bond to the narrator that would not otherwise exist.

This tale truly encompasses a bit of everything, ranging from topics as wholesome as childhood nostalgia and laughter, to ones as horrific as illness and abuse. Many of the themes encountered throughout the story are life-oriented and broad, which makes the book relatable to all sorts of people from different walks of life. There is much to be learned from the manner in which Patty perceives and manages these easily relatable topics, including education, family, and health.

Early on, you will discover the important role that education plays in her life, and how this passion represents something positive that she can focus on and dream about, while simultaneously preventing her from revisiting the negative elements of her past. Becoming a teacher also allows her the opportunity to travel and meet new friends, many of whom wind up lending her the love and support that her family did not. It is widely acknowledged that finding a passion in life is important, but Patty is able to contribute a whole new layer to this message, by highlighting the healing properties that her particular passion was able to bring her.

She has spent most of her life excelling as a teacher, yet it is possible that Patty's most impactful lesson has yet to be taught and lies within these pages. Coming from circumstances as drastic and dire as facing parental abuse and neglect, to accomplishing one of the crowning honors in life (receiving a doctoral degree), the breadth of Patty's experiences can be rivaled by very few others, if any. This makes her the ideal conduit to inspire encouragement and fortitude in others. Patty's toughness is without question, one of her most admirable attributes, and it is a compelling and emotional privilege to watch her fiercely defy the predetermined path that life seemed so eager to thrust her down.

As you read on, and as Patty arms herself with the right tools to conquer the damning nature of her past, a sense of hope begins to shine through the pages, becoming more and more luminous with each turn of the page. Not only hope that the narrator will be able to overcome the obstacles in her life but hope towards our own lives and circumstances—hope that by using the very same tools that she did, we can construct our own divine path, and create the life that we want for ourselves. However, as I finished the story, I came to realize that there was no longer a need for such hope. After all, hope only exists for things that are uncertain. And Patty's life experience has taught me that one thing is for sure: *No matter where you start from, or what life throws your way, it is entirely possible to control your own destiny.* Doctor Wyman is living proof of this.

Introduction

I
s it possible for an individual to control her own destiny, no matter what obstacles life presents? How does she recover from being torn away from her parents and childhood home? Can she ever trust and experience a normal relationship after being molested by someone she thought was supposed to be her protector? This is an account of my life and how I deliberately chose to survive several traumatic events starting at a very early age. It includes key factors in my own individual methods of coping and controlling my life path.

This story is meant to inform family and friends of my life events. I don't want to be the person who hides everything from others. I especially want my children to know my herstory, medical experiences and conditions, and the narrative of my severely dysfunctional family. At the same time, it is a personal account of recollections, anecdotes, and fun nostalgic tales of my past. This reminiscent journey is a cathartic experience that allows the readers, and me, to recognize what inspired me to become exactly the person I am today. Educators and education had major impact on my survival and eventual success. The story also discusses the significant roles played by friends, who unknowingly helped me to survive and to find happiness on a day-to-day basis.

It is my hope that this autobiography inspires others to believe that they, too, can choose the direction of their own futures. Of course, if the readers enjoy this trip down memory lane while learning more about me, then that's all the better. This book is open and honest, to the very best of my recollections. People who already know me may read some things they consider annoying or even disturbing. That's okay. I will still be exactly the same person they already knew before reading my story.

Chapter 1

A Rough Start

We are not doomed to repeat our past,
unless we choose to do so.
~William Glasser~

Perhaps I should just begin. One thing is certain, if I don't write it, this story will never be told by anyone. Born on December 21, 1950, just four days before the biggest holiday of the year, I was a gift to my family. At least that's what my mother said many years later. She claimed I came home, wrapped in a big red bow on Christmas Day, from St. Joseph Hospital in Lorain, Ohio. I was taken a short distance to 245 Fay Avenue, our home in Avon Lake and lived there from birth to age four. I do not recall much from my first four years of life. However, a few early memories do emerge.

Animals have always been important to me because they provide a pure unconditional love. Prior to age four, I know that we briefly had a very tall greyhound dog and then a German shepherd that I loved. I don't re-member their names or any other details, but I do recall them in my young life. The fact that I remember those dogs at all, from such an early age, speaks to the significance that animals play in my life.

Then, there was one very frightening early memory. Sometime around age three I was stubborn enough to refuse to take "No!" for an answer. My mother was drinking hot tea and I wanted a cup, but she justly refused. So, I decided to make my own. I boldly stood up to the stove on a high stool, which proved to be disastrous. I spilled the boiling hot water all over myself. I remember running, room to room, screaming and crying. I was hospitalized for a long time in a children's burn unit. Three vivid memories of that hospital stay stand out for me.

On one visit I was given a brand-new doll by my parents. There was a little Black kid named Jackie in my room. He was so sad and cried most of the time. So, I gave Jackie my new doll. Of course, my parents did not understand my overly empathetic nature at such an early age. They were not at all pleased with my act of kindness. I was later told by my half-sister, Gail, that both parents were old school racists, so that complicated matters even more. My family teased me about that for many years.

In my hospital room, I would lie awake for what seemed like hours in a crib-type bed. I watched the reflections from the car lights dancing upon the upper walls. We must have been facing the road or the parking lot because they seemed never-ending. Eventually, those reflections helped me to fall asleep. When I see car light reflections today, I am reminded of being in that medical facility so long ago.

Whatever they did at that hospital seemed to be highly successful. I was quite fortunate to have no permanent scarring. I clearly recall the ride home when I was finally discharged. My mother, father, little brother, Frankie, and I were all in the backseat of a taxi. Frankie was only a little over one year old and that day, he had a big cut under his left eye. They told me he fell and hit his cheekbone on a paint can, so he had to have stitches. That big scar stayed on his face until he died. I thought it was my fault because I was not at home to take care of my baby brother.

Funny, I just spoke with my older half-brother, Howard, recently. I hadn't talked to him in years. I learned a few interesting facts about our time in Avon Lake. Howard is eleven years older than me. He and Bruce were full brothers to Gail and Barbara. According to Howard, he and his brother left our home to live with their father, Mr. Coleman, and a very mean stepmother in Columbia Station, Ohio. To the best of his knowledge, that happened in 1953. I was only three then. That's right around the same time I was burned.

Howard said he got along fairly well with my father, Frank Sr., but our mother, May, was the one who used physical discipline. Once she took a two-by-four to one of those boys. It's probably best I don't remember our mother's wrath. However, it does make me wonder if Frankie really fell over a paint can.

The thing Howard clearly remembers about my father is that he absolutely loved St. Patrick's Day. I know he repeatedly made sure we knew we were Irish. He used to tell us that his real name was Francis Joseph Patrick Aloysius Bohner Sr. and we believed him. It makes sense that St. Patrick's Day was his favorite holiday. He loved to drink every chance he had, usually, all day long. Every day was St. Patrick's Day for him.

The year after I burned myself, we were taken out of that "family" home by the Lorain County Welfare Department. Apparently, my oldest half-sister, Gail, was around twelve years old when she was caught robbing a private residence with a few of her friends. Her arrest was just the catalyst to our removal from that "unsafe home." Sometime before that, my other sister, Fran had almost drowned when she fell off a fishing pier on Lake Erie. The story is that a priest jumped into the water to save her. Our parents were both alcoholics who enjoyed partying more than taking care of their kids. According to the County Welfare, we were "neglected" and had run up and down the neighborhood dirty and naked just one too many times. The neighbors complained. Apparently, I must have felt a need to clean up my act. I chopped my long hair into a pixie style right before we were removed from our home. Don't most little kids cut their hair at some point in time?

CHAPTER 2

Living in a Foster Home

If you're going through hell, keep going.
~Winston Churchill~

Five of us were escorted away from our parents by the police and county workers. My two older half-brothers had already left to live with their father. I have no memory of them being with us. The rest of us were immediately moved to a foster home. Now we had to live at 839 Reid Ave. in Lorain, Ohio, where I stayed ages four through nine. My two half-sisters, Gail, and Barbara were there with us. We shared the same mother but had different fathers. Gail (twelve years), and Barbara (eight), were both Colemans; as were their two older brothers, Howard, and Bruce. My sister, Fran (age six), Frankie (two), and I (four) were Bohners. Our mother, May, and father, Frank Sr., were married, and we were taken from them. Strange, but each child held very different views regarding how we experienced that same foster home. Maybe it was about perception, due to our age variation. Regardless, Gertrude Fisher, "Aunt Gert" and Roy Fisher, "Uncle Roy" were our new foster parents for the next five years.

Not once in those five years did anyone ever discuss why we were no longer living in Avon Lake with our mother and father. Somehow, that didn't bother me. I was too young to care and tended to live day-to-day. I didn't know anything about why we were removed from our home until nearly thirty-five years later, when our mother died. That's when my two half-sisters knew I was trying to get answers about my early life so they told me as much as they could remember through phone calls and letters. They always blamed our mother and felt that she had neglected them. None of us kids had any love for our mother.

Aunt Gert, our foster mother, was extremely strict and not at all hesitant to dole out punishments. She claimed it hurt her more than it hurt us. I frankly doubt that! If we cried, she said "Stop that crying or I'll give you something to really cry about." I'm sweaty and nervous now just thinking about how much we all hated when people gifted us with those wooden paddle toys. They came with a long string and an attached rubber ball. You were supposed to enjoy hitting the ball repeatedly with the paddle but ours never made it that far. Aunt Gert immediately pulled the ball and rubber band cord off and armed herself with paddles for spanking us. Now that I am much older, I feel overwhelmed when I consider how hard it must have been for our foster mother to care for all five of us at once. Guess she was kind of an "evil saint." Now that's an oxymoron if I ever heard one!

Most of the time, I wasn't even aware of how mean our foster mother really was. I didn't get into trouble very often because I tried to please people at that young age. My older half-sisters told me they thought of me as their little angel. In all my years, I have never seen myself that way. I do know that I absolutely tried to take care of my toddler brother and was dubbed "Little Mother" by Aunt Gert. I felt sorry for Frankie because he was so young and the only boy living with four sisters.

I don't remember too much from that first year of foster living. I do recall that four of us slept sideways in a double bed. Gail, the oldest, had her own bedroom, which I later learned was so that she could "entertain" Uncle Roy privately. At some point I remember learning the word "cooperate" from him because he repeatedly told the other kids that I would not cooperate. Roy actually built a private loft area in the garage, with plywood planks, where he attempted to "cuddle" with us. It was especially bad when he went to town for a haircut and came back smelling like alcohol. Sometimes Roy would shove me into Gail's bedroom closet and close the door behind him. I refused to allow him to do anything to me and told him I would scream if he didn't let me out. I secretly hated that man!

I remember being terrified at bath time. I always thought Uncle Roy would come in when I was in the tub, so I usually faked my bath if I was alone. We were not allowed to lock the doors. I didn't get into the tub. I just stood by the sink and faced the door while I filled the tub. Then I splashed water on myself—especially on my hair and ears before emptying the tub. Aunt Gert never failed to check our ears after a bath. I protected myself and got away with it.

Uncle Roy worked in the Lorain Steelyard during the week. On the weekends he usually took us on long rides "in the country" for an hour or two. He had a nice big green Chevy with a shiny chrome bumper grill on the front end. Roy took us places like the Elyria Park, where I remember they had a giant Easter basket out front on the grass. I saw it all the time on my bus ride to school. We also spent time at Cascade Park. I loved that tall scary spiral slide. Uncle Roy liked taking us to the Lorain County Fair. We enjoyed seeing all the animals and the "side show freaks." Even the name is far from being politically correct; let alone putting actual humans with differences on display and charging money to do so. We thought it was fun then.

I loved having our older sisters living in the foster home. They really watched out and took care of the rest of us. However, I was often mad at Gail. She took Frankie fishing with her. I wanted to get out, too. When they left, I usually cried, but she never once took me. She said fishing was for boys so my brother could go fishing because he was a boy. I was very confused and called out an injustice way back then. She was a girl! That did not make sense.

I believe that's one reason why I loved school so much. It gave me the chance to get away from home. I do fondly recall my very first day of kindergarten. I wore a pea green dress with very cool Snapjack saddle shoes. They had spring-loaded closures, so I didn't have to tie them. It was pouring down rain and I had to take a bus to school in Elyria, which turned into a nightmare for me. It was about a thirty-minute bus ride. Irving Elementary in Lorain did not have a kindergarten at that time. I memorized the house where the bus picked me up. Unfortunately, it dropped me off on the opposite side of the street. It was not the "right house!" I refused to get off and ended up at the bus terminal at the end of the line. A station manager took me home twice. Luckily for me, on the third day, two of my sisters walked by just as I was arguing yet again with the bus driver that it was not my stop. I still recall my sisters staring and laughing until one of them finally yelled, "Get off the bus, STUPID!" Finally, someone explained the situation of pickup versus return to me. It was just the wrong side of the street! The perception of a five-year-old can be quite interesting. A lot of us had *Amelia Bedelia* literal type of thinking at that age.

Another horrible problem I had with the bus experience was when I lost my token to get on the bus. A classmate, Ruth, lived close to the bus stop so she ran home to get me a token. The bus came and the driver had to wait for her, so she got in trouble. I also was punished because I was the one who asked Ruth to get me the token so that Aunt Gert wouldn't be mad at me. That idea didn't work out the way I had hoped. I definitely got in trouble in spite of trying to avoid it.

On another occasion, Ruth was again late for the bus. She lied and said it was my fault, so her mother immediately called Aunt Gert. This time I was at home and sick in bed, so it was obvious Ruth was not telling the truth. From then on, I was not allowed to play with Ruth.

I had other friends to play with. Some kids that I still remember to this day are Ricky Smith, Edna, Judy, and our neighbor, Johnnie. Ricky was really a "bad boy" in school. He was in trouble nearly every minute and spent most of his time sitting on the floor, right next to the teacher's rocking chair. It never bothered him. He just faced us kids and made crazy faces all day. I remember he had short hair and big ears that he could wiggle! Edna was the tallest child in our class and had very frizzy, long red hair. Edna was very nice to everyone. I really liked Judy because she was so beautiful. Her dad was a doctor and she had pretty clothes and a shiny long dark ponytail. Her sister was in Fran's class. Then there was also Carol, who came to the house frequently with her mom, Aunt Gert's friend. Right down the alley from our house was Johnnie. He's probably a chemist or a comedian today. Johnnie was always putting salt in the sugar jar or mixing other ingredients into people's Kool-aide, to get a reaction.

One tragic memory I have from our neighborhood is when a man who lived across the street, kitty-cornered from us, committed suicide. We didn't have any idea what that meant, but we heard all the adults whispering about how Floyd died while leaving his car running in the garage. It really is strange what memories are etched into our brains forever.

That was around the same time Aunt Gert's friend brought a young boy over and took us kids to a movie. For some reason, I do not have any idea what the movie was, but someone was eating dirt. We thought that was pretty funny, but the young boy sitting with us started crying and said he remembered when he had to eat dirt. Aunt Gert later explained he had lived in a concentration camp during the Holocaust. In our very sheltered lives, we had absolutely no idea what that was all about.

I remember when our parents came to visit us in the foster home. Somehow, our mother, May, lost visiting privileges when she repeatedly became agitated or irate. May often showed up at random times, without an appointment. On several occasions, our distraught mother attempted to take us home with her, but she was always stopped. May usually had to be escorted away by the police. The terrifying picture of a mother pulled away from her children sticks in a kid's head. Those scenes with the police were always intense and scary. I imagine that's when I began to see May as the bad guy. We really didn't want to see her at all. Ultimately, my mother suffered a nervous breakdown and had electrical shock treatments. From then on, we could only have supervised visits with her at the County Welfare Agency. If she wanted to be outside with us, we had to go out in the parking lot with a social worker to watch over us. I still remember one case worker we liked, Mr. Steffencheck, because he treated us kindly. We didn't see May for an awfully long time and then suddenly she had a new baby sister for us to meet in the parking lot! Little May, named after our mother, was adorable. At some point she was also taken from our mother, just as we were. But Little May was immediately adopted out as a baby by the county welfare agency. I never saw my baby sister again. Luckily, we somehow had a photo of that gathering.

Then, there were visits with our father, Frank Sr., who always got to play the "good guy" role. He brought us presents and saw us for a few hours many weekends, and most holidays. In due time, he was allowed to take us on outings like the circus, Cedar Point, or Chippewa and Geauga Lakes. One Christmas when our father came to visit, Fran and I received Wanda, the Walking Dolls! When you wound up a key on the huge eighteen-inch doll she moved her head, arms, and legs. We loved those dolls. Unfortunately, I remember announcing that night that it wasn't such a bad Christmas after all. Aunt Gert was deeply hurt by my comment. She felt she had done so much to give us a nice Christmas. Then our father drops in with a big doll and he's the hero. That's the first time I was aware of hurting someone's feelings.

We had a big old coal furnace in the foster home. One of our favorite activities was to watch the men on delivery days. A big dump truck backed into our yard and pulled up to the shoot on the side of the house. There, they dumped coal on a slide-like plank right into the coal cellar of the basement. That coal furnace gave off great heat! We loved sitting on a hassock over the heat register while Aunt Gert made dinner. One time my father had given me a tiny toy piano for Christmas. Every night I would sit on that floor register at the window with my little piano. I made up a song about my daddy coming to pick me up after work. It was a big hit when he came to visit.

Toward the end of our foster stay, when our father came for a visitation, he introduced us to a woman named Kay, and her son, Ronnie. He took us all together on some of those outings. We didn't realize it, but she was soon to be his wife and our new stepmother.

I remember one Christmas our father was allowed to take us from the foster home to a party at his friend, Zeke's house. I was so happy because I got a brand-new Shirley Temple doll. Then suddenly I wasn't happy, but very frightened. We were crying because the adults were all inebriated and an argument broke out. I had honestly never remembered seeing drunk people or actual physical violence before. Earlier, in Avon Lake, when my parents were drinking and fighting, I was too young to remember it. There were a lot of bad words and yelling. The teen boy, I think his name was Butch, ended up knocking over the Christmas tree and broken glass bulbs flew everywhere. Our father said if we told anyone he wouldn't be allowed to see us ever again. Of course, we never told one person.

We stayed in that foster home for five long years—all five of us together. I loved Aunt Gert's cooking and baking. She made the best fudge, popcorn balls, hot buttered rolls, and on Easter, a special coconut lamb cake. Each morning, she made us swallow a spoonful of Castor Oil. I still don't know what that was for. We just heard that "Franny was too skinny and needed to be fattened up." The only foods I really disliked were liver, homemade applesauce, and any kind of pudding. Liver was just gross! Applesauce and pudding had too many lumps. And I couldn't take that slimy skin on top of the pudding.

We had to stay at the dining table until our plates were clean because of some "starving kids in China." Whenever we had any of those three foods, I was always the last one at the table. As everyone took their plate to the kitchen, I wrapped the food into my paper napkin and put it in my pants. When I was finally dismissed, I headed straight to the bathroom and flushed it down the toilet. I am surprised I never flooded it. I still don't eat liver, pudding, or any creme-type foods today. Finally, after 60 plus years, I did try adding applesauce to a muffin recipe. It wasn't as terrible as I thought.

The Fishers, my foster parents, had a black and white dog named Rex. Once again, I was able to feel unconditional love. Caring for animals was a way for me to escape into a positive world. Animals never treated me badly. Rex played with us and let us bathe him or brush his long fur. He was a good dog and appreciated our hugs. We used to get paid a nickel to take napkins and a paper bag out back to clean up after him. I guess that was really my very first job. We also got paid to pick up cigarette butts in the yard. I remember picking up Uncle Roy's cigarette filters and sucking the nicotine out of them every time I found them outside. He smoked Salem Menthols. In addition to Rex, we had two pet bunnies that lived in the garage. One time they tore a hole in their cage and were found sitting on our bicycle seats. We thought that was the funniest thing we had ever seen.

Our foster home was on a main street right between a gas station and a huge Jewish Temple. We learned to ride our brand-new bikes over at the gas station parking lot when I was eight years old. All five of us got new bikes on the same day! Us kids appreciated when the Temple hosted big parties. That meant the next day would bring happy dumpster diving for us! We would pull out streamers, balloons, and colorful paper products from the trash. Then we would dress up to parade all around the Temple steps in our roller skates. It's amazing we never killed ourselves, as the expandable skates rarely fit properly over our shoes. Somehow those skate keys never really worked.

Our foster mother, Aunt Gert, had two sides to her personality. I don't recall her ever going out of the house, except when she went on the front porch. She could be totally fun when she wasn't mad at us. We loved Saturdays when American Bandstand came on the old black and white television set. We pushed all the living room furniture aside and danced and laughed our silliness out. Sometimes our foster mother even danced with us.

Saturday was also the day Aunt Gert rewarded us. We all had to show her our hands for a fingernail inspection. That's when we earned a nickel for every nail that had a "moon" on the cuticle, or at the base of our nailbeds, because that represented a healthy nail. Fran was really quite good at that and earned a lot of nickels. I rarely ever got any money because I was a thumb sucker and a nail biter. Haha! I just now remembered that Fran used to suck two fingers together instead of her thumb. I guess she quit so she could collect moons. It wasn't so easy for me. Aunt Gert tried covering my thumb with nasty tasting things like bitters, hot sauce, tabasco, Vaseline, and even Band-Aids. Nothing got between that right thumb and me. I recall being traumatized by those nail inspections and developed a serious fear. I thought that something would get me if any of my fingernails or toenails were outside from under the blankets at night. Perception is everything at an early age.

Our well-earned nickels were kept in a little medicine bottle "bank." Wow! Now that makes me wonder why there were so many bottles and what meds Gert, or Roy were taking. I know that at one point they tried to formally adopt all of us. They were denied, due to their ages of late fifties or early sixties, and for health reasons. All I remember about Gert's health was that "hot dogs didn't like her." That's what she said when I asked why she didn't like hot dogs.

But when Gert was angry, she was extremely angry. There was a time that my sister, Barbara and I received inhumane punishment for something that was honestly innocent. With no air conditioning or fans in the bedroom, one summer night we were especially hot. We took our jammies off to try and cool down. Aunt Gert came into our room. She had a scary way of storming into the room late at night when we were just about asleep. This time, I guess we told on ourselves as we were giggling and had the sheets pulled completely up to our necks. She stripped back those sheets and went on a rage about how we were committing such terrible sins. Seriously? We were simply trying to cool down. So innocent! Regardless, the next day we had to stand in opposite corners of the playroom totally naked! I recall our friend, Carol, and her mother came by and were just shocked to see how we were being disciplined. We had to stay there most of the day, until dinner time when I likely got into trouble again for not eating my pudding! Yeah, maybe I didn't realize it day-to-day, but now that I honestly think about it, Gert could be extremely mean sometimes.

I recently learned of another horrible discipline episode regarding Aunt Gert. I have no personal memory of this, but in a letter, Barbara said that Aunt Gert used an evil method of potty-training Frankie. When he had an accident, she dressed him in one of my skirts and told all of us to shame him. We had to do it because we were terrified of her wrath.

The first time I recalled one of my dreams it got me into a lot of trouble. I dreamt that all of us kids were sitting on a bed while Aunt Gert told us a scary story about the neighborhood Boogeyman. I can still see him clearly– a tall slim man dressed in all black. He had long shaggy hair and a big beard. He wore a black top hat just like Frosty, the Snowman, and a long black coat with tails. The Boogeyman scared the crap out of me! I pictured Aunt Gert pulling back the second-floor corner bedroom curtain ever so slightly to make each of us peek out to see him standing down there. There he was, right across the street under a streetlamp! She had always warned us that the Boogeyman would take us away if we didn't behave.

Aunt Gert was livid with me and denied ever telling us such a story. According to her, it just never happened. It was all a dream! Hard lesson learned there: Do not talk about my dreams. It sure seemed real to me and I honestly thought that's exactly how it happened. I don't remember my specific punishment for telling a lie that day, but I do know that often when Aunt Gert was frustrated with us, she would say things like "I should just give you back to the Indians." I thought I was an Indian for the longest time. Or she would say, "Go outside and get the stink off you!"

Gert and Roy were not religious people, but I never once heard either of them swear. Instead, she would yell, "Jesus, Mary, and Joseph!" They didn't go to church, but she dressed all five of us up and sent us to St. Mary's Catholic Church just down the street. We liked going to church because we got away and felt a little independent. We could never leave the house on Sundays without a fresh red and white round peppermint. I guess we all had bad breath.

We enjoyed church so much that Fran went through the steps to complete her First Communion ceremony. She even had the beautiful white dress, shoes and socks, with a long sheer veil. She also had a tiny, purse-sized mother of pearl Bible for her special day. Our Godfather was supposed to be a guy named Ernie Kerstine, our father's friend. He was an FBI agent and I believe we only met him once. I don't think he was really our Godfather. Suddenly, the day before the ceremony the social worker found out. He stopped the entire process. He said our foster parents had no right to choose a religion for us. The County Court had to give approval for something like that. Fran was obviously devastated. I don't remember if we ever went back to that church again. We had to question the whole idea of God, church, and the reasons why such a thing could happen. Instead, we used Fran's Communion outfit to play dress up, like for our bride and groom weddings. We had a little side garden next to the big brick wall of the Temple. That's where we held pretend weddings and circuses.

Every Easter us kids were really decked out. Of course, everything was hand sewn whenever possible. Aunt Gert had real talent and a great Singer sewing machine. She made our slips, shorts, skirts, pants, shirts, and even coats. But on Easter she went all out. We wore white patent leather shoes with white ruffled socks, a frilly dress which often had a stiff hoop slip underneath to make it very puffy, and a full-length button-down coat. Of course, the outfits wouldn't be complete without white cotton gloves, a little purse, and a beautiful Easter bonnet.

One day in kindergarten, we made our own Easter bonnets from paper plates. They were decorated with all sorts of bright objects. Our teacher brought her pet bunny into class and I loved holding that cute little guy. He was so cuddly and warm. I was chosen to be on the front page of *The Lorain Beacon Journal* wearing my paper plate hat while holding that bunny. I was so proud and felt special.

Aunt Gert made the best costumes for us. We became whomever we chose to be—gypsies, pirates, cowgirls, hobos, *Bandstand* dancers with poodle skirts, pilgrims, Indians, witches, or ghosts. We dressed up for birthday parties, holidays, and masquerade parties. We even had long pioneer dresses with matching bonnets for Lorain's Sesquicentennial Celebration. I don't know about the other kids, but I always loved the outfits Aunt Gert made for us.

One scary day I recall during our foster home stay was when all five of us kids walked into town. It was only about two blocks away—down the alley and one block over. Somehow, we all became distracted and lost Frankie in the dime store. We panicked and told the store manager we separated from our little brother. He called home and we knew we were in big trouble. Finally, when we arrived home Aunt Gert was waiting at the top of the front porch steps. She was kind of smiling and we didn't understand why she wasn't screaming at us. Then out from behind her peeked our little brother. He said, "Where were you guys? You guys got lost!" Frankie had walked home all by himself. It was a long time before we were allowed to go to town again.

Another time, I thought Aunt Gert would kill me was when she caught me stealing. Her usual "middle of the night" rage happened once again. It was kind of like the Joan Crawford hanger scenes in the movie, *Mommie Dearest*. She threw the light switch on and pulled me out of bed screaming that she had found money in my coat pockets. Aunt Gert demanded to know where that money came from. I had taken the money from her purse. When my friend, Carol, and I went into town to run an errand for Aunt Gert, we stopped in the 5 and 10 store. I treated Carol to a Coke at the counter. Sitting on the high stools, sipping ice-cold drinks, made me feel happy, like a bigshot. Unfortunately, Carol told her mother about the Coke.

I also stole money to buy Luden's Wild Cherry Cough Drops for my whole kindergarten class. We were repeatedly told we could not eat in class unless we had enough to share with everybody. So, I handed out one cherry cough drop to each classmate. When Aunt Gert confronted me, I fessed up. I may have been at the receiving end of more than one wooden paddle that time.

Truthfully, it didn't stop me from stealing. I recall taking two York Peppermint Patties from my kindergarten teacher's desk. As we marched around the perimeter of our classroom while banging on our toy instruments, I snatched the candy. I shoved both patties into my mouth and threw the crumpled wrappers on the chalk tray as I marched past. No one caught me! When the teacher asked who took the candies from her desk, I never even looked in her direction. If she had checked our mouths or tongues, I'm sure she would have found chocolate on mine. Or if she asked me, I would likely have told the truth. But she never did either and I wasn't going to volunteer that confession.

As I look back, I see that I was no "angel," but I wasn't really a bad kid either. Guess I would classify myself more as a curious, mischievous little kid. Once my curiosity got the best of me though. Again, in kindergarten, I must have come across as a dependable child. I was honored with the most trusted classroom job on the list. I was picked to be the "Messenger." My job was to take all communications for my teacher to, and from, the office. One day I was going all the way down to the office by myself to deliver our classroom attendance folder. Everything was fine until I hit the bottom step and saw the little red "FIRE" box with the pulldown handle. It's not like it was premeditated or anything, but for whatever reason, I had to pull that lever. It clanged so loudly it scared the heck out of me. I ran into the office where they immediately escorted me outside. Everything happened so fast! The entire school was going outside and suddenly we heard sirens. Firefighters in huge firetrucks showed up. They checked the school building and after a while, gave everyone the all-clear to reenter. No one had any idea as to who pulled that alarm. Of course, I didn't say a word. I was terrified!

The next day I was called to the office. I was sure I was in very serious trouble. Wrong! One of the clerks looked at me and asked, "When you brought the attendance down yesterday, did you see any boys out in the hallway?" I thought that was an odd question. After telling them that I saw no one in the hall they thanked me and let me go back to my classroom. I never told anyone about that incident until I was in college. There, I feel much better just confessing and am no longer embarrassed. I was just a little kid!

Another time in kindergarten I felt really humiliated. I had colored an entire workbook page red. I was uncomfortable when our teacher held up the book and said, "We have one special artist in this class. She loves the color red. Everything on her page is red but look how she stayed in all the lines. Right now, her face is very red!" I wanted to crawl into a hole. Suddenly I just remembered I even had to have a red rug in kindergarten for naptime. I think that incident marked the very day I changed my favorite color to orange.

CHAPTER 3

Living with My Father

I have a feeling we're not in Kansas anymore.
~Dorothy~
"Wizard of Oz"

So, my father married that woman who went to the amusement parks with us. He did so because the court ordered him to do three things to gain custody of his children. He had to be married, provide a home, and have separate bedrooms for the males and females. We moved to 3447 Cypress Avenue in Cleveland, Ohio, which was right off State Road. I lived there from ages nine to seventeen. The house was a huge, old, side-by-side duplex. On the other side of the duplex lived the Grycan family. Mike and Idell were the parents. June, Marilyn, and Margaret were the kids. Marilyn, who was Mern to us, was my age and became one of my best friends. Our friendship wasn't always smooth sailing. That was mostly because I was forever trying to change her. I wanted her to have a "better" life. Now I realize that was a better life, according to my standards, not hers. In spite of that, we were lifelong friends until the very end; sixty-one years! We had lots of adventures together. I honestly tried for years to get Mern to coauthor a book with me called "Living in a Duplex." I wanted it to be so exciting that we would be on the Oprah Show. That's something I had hoped to achieve so I would know I was successful. It never happened. My success will have to be measured in another way.

Moving to Cleveland on January 30, 1960, was a bag of mixed emotions. To begin with, we had to leave our older half-sister, Barbara, behind in the foster home. That was painful, especially since it was her fourteenth birthday. As we drove away, Gert Fisher told Barbara that she would never be our sister again. Barbara was miserable in that foster home all alone. She ended up also leaving the Fisher's and went to another foster home just five months after we moved out. The Fishers punished her by not allowing Barbara to take her bicycle or the new ice skates she had received for her birthday. Somehow, Fran ended up with those skates. She probably got them during the only time we visited the Fishers, less than a year after we left. Funny, they quickly replaced us with five new foster kids by then.

Gail had already moved out of our foster home the previous year. She was seventeen and had been abused long enough! She went to a new foster home with the Schmidtkins, who lived on a large fruit farm. Gail seemed very happy with her new family. I remember visiting that farm when she graduated from nursing school.

Naively, I had absolutely no idea what was in store for me in Cleveland. I just knew I was excited to finally have a "real family." Now the three of us, Fran, Frank, and I, lived with our father, a stepmother, and a stepbrother. From day one, our stepmother, Kay, openly favored her son. Ronnie was already spoiled by his mother. The whole thing was very awkward with no emotional connection. We could see immediately that we were not going to be that happy family I had dreamt about while in the foster home. Fran and I spent most of that first day upstairs, setting up our bedroom. Ronnie kept barging in and bothering us. That boy, Ronnie, could do no wrong in his mother's eyes. He lied about everything and she accepted it. Kay never believed us if we tried to tell her some of the bad things he did. She basically tolerated us but loved her son. I wasn't at all prepared for that. My expectations were way out of line. Kay had always been sweet when all of us went on outings with our father before they were married. Suddenly it seemed like we were intruders who were dumped on her. She definitely had no love for us.

On the very first day in Cleveland my beautiful bike was stolen from out in front of the house. My stepmother blamed me and said it was my own fault because I didn't take care of the bike. It was a long time before I ever got another one, but we quickly learned all about locks and chains. I had a lot to understand about Cleveland.

One of the first games we played with our new neighbors was Monsters in the Basement. The duplex shared a door in the basement that led to both halves of the house. It was a huge basement with a laundry area, canning rooms, and big ledges under the windows. We could only use flashlights to get around and scare each other. We knew we were quite successful if Mern's little sister, Margaret, peed her pants! That was our fright barometer. We sure loved that scary game!

Mern and I enjoyed hiding anywhere. We liked being away from everything and everyone. One of our favorite hideaways was the crawl space under the front or back porch. We sat in the dirt and just peeked out at everyone through the porch lattice. From the front we saw all the bar action. From the back we saw the beverage store customers.

But our favorite hiding spot was high in the treetops. We positively preferred climbing trees and would go as high as we possibly could without breaking a branch. Sometimes we sat up there for hours just laughing and talking because we felt safe in our hideaway. We enjoyed finding different types of trees to climb. Once we were trespassing in a yard across the street so we could climb new trees. Someone yelled, "COPS!" We all ran as fast as we could. All except Mern, who was still up in a tree! Everyone abandoned her and she ended up sliding straight down the trunk of the tree, scraping up her entire belly and chest area. Mern was mad at us, for at least as long as it took her torn-up belly to heal.

Eventually that same house on our street, where we trespassed, was rented out by a guy named Paul Bruno. He was a nightclub singer who did cover songs. Bruno was divorced and lived by himself, but we went to school with two of his seven kids: Paula and Terri. Bruno was extremely handsome and had a great voice. We loved when he let us sit in on practice sessions before his evening performances. Sometime when we were in junior high, Paul Bruno was sentenced to life in prison for first degree murder. He was found guilty of shooting a Cleveland mobster, Joseph Horay, in the head after a bar fight. So, at the young age of thirty-six he was imprisoned for the rest of his life. Too bad! We actually liked the guy because he was nice to us.

At age ten, our stepbrother, Ronnie, taught us a great deal. He introduced us to the idea of sex, demonstrating with our little action figures. He taught us an endless list of swear words that we had never heard. He just tried to teach us as many bad things as he could, as quickly as he was able. One time he had me write a note calling Mern's mother a whore. I didn't know what that meant, but I put the note in her mailbox without questioning it. Of course, I was the one who got in trouble for that little prank. Ronnie even convinced us to have a "Grycan Haters Club" when Mern was my best friend. He said they had cooties. I think that was around the time June threw a dart that stuck in Fran's butt.

Ronnie ran around the house jumping off the furniture, beating on his chest, and screaming like Tarzan. My father always called him "Little Lord Fauntleroy." I really had no idea why he called him that. Sometimes I was entertained by Ronnie and sometimes I thought he was absolutely crazy. I really started to dislike him when he punched me in the mouth and chipped my front teeth. I recall my father coming home and just saying,

"Those are her permanent teeth." I didn't understand the comment or why Ronnie didn't get punished. He never seemed to get into trouble with either adult. I was mad because I really wanted Ronnie to be in hot water. Those front teeth are still chipped today.

Ronnie was a year ahead of me at Dawning Elementary School when I moved to Cleveland in grade three. I still remember going to my new school and being introduced to the class. We started long division on my first day there. The teacher, Miss Dufresne, turned to me and said, "Don't worry if this is hard for you. I'll help you." She was shocked when she saw that I understood the process and caught on faster than the rest of the kids. I recall her comment was something about never having a student move in the middle of the year and being ahead of her class. All I did was repeat the process she had just shown us. I liked how she explained it and found the steps easy to follow.

The next year Ronnie and I ended up in a fourth-grade class together because he failed. Back then we had Groups A and B. One group moved ahead in January and the other in June. He was only in my room for one semester. We had different last names, so I hardly ever told anyone we were related. During that time, he really hated me because I loved school and did well. He didn't! Then he went to summer school and caught up with his own class. Thank goodness because I really hated him, too.

CHAPTER 4

Cleveland Relatives

Your life will get better when you realize it's better to be alone
than chase people who don't really care about you.
~Thema Davis~

Ronnie had a little cousin, Debbie, who came to visit us often. She was much younger and a sweet little kid. Her father was Carl, the brother of our stepmother, Kay. Carl liked us and was so good to us Bohner kids. He came over at least weekly with Debbie. His wife, Evelyn, rarely ever visited us. All the adults drank beer and smoked. They had strong cigarettes back then like Camels, Pall Mall, or Lucky Strike with no filters. Kay was different. She smoked Kool Menthols. Carl made cigarette runs to the store and took us for rides in his car on hot summer nights, just so we could cool down. I loved sticking my head out the car window and staring at the ground passing by so quickly until I was dizzy. Carl was just one of the good guys.

My father, Frank Sr., had a brother, my Uncle Art Bohner. He was one of my favorite relatives. Uncle Art often stuck up for us when we got yelled at. His wife, Mary, came over all the time. She felt a need to interfere in our lives under the pretense of helping. We named her "Mary, the Fairy." She was always fluttering about, sticking her nose where it didn't belong. She usually brought us some sort of food as an excuse to pop in. Mary taught me how to do laundry. I constantly got my fingers caught in that old-fashioned wringer washer. I hated it because it terrified me! Aunt Mary also showed me how to iron clothes. I can still see her sprinkling water on the clean dry clothes because we didn't have a steam iron. Then she flipped over the button side of the shirts and unfolded the collar fully before pressing it flat. She did the same thing with the button cuffs. I guess Mary did teach me some good things. That's about it for people who came to visit on a regular basis.

Our mother didn't visit. She wasn't welcomed by our father. He never said much about May except he made fun of her hair. He said she always had a different hair color each time she picked us up. Guess that alone speaks for how rarely we saw her. Our father and mother weren't on speaking terms, probably because he took full custody of us. I do know that a while back she had claimed he was the father of her eighth child, Little May, who was born a few years after their divorce. She wanted child support from him. He denied it and had to go to court. In the end, a paternity test proved he was right. Little May wasn't his child.

Of course, our mother wasn't allowed to come and see us at our house. If she wanted a visit, she took us briefly on a couple of busses to her mother's home, which I think was somewhere near Storer Ave. Sometimes our mother would take us to see her sister, my Aunt Flo, who was just so happy and full of life. I recall attending several holiday parties down in Aunt Flo and Uncle Bob Tonne's basement. Her kids Chuckie, Bobby, Tammy, and Sherry were great kids and fun cousins. We just never saw them very often.

Aunt Flo loved the beach and the sunshine! She taught us how to get a great suntan out in the backyard. Mern and I loved sunning up on the business roof next door to our duplex. We held our little pocket transistor radios up to our ears to hear the latest rock-n-roll. We spread out a little blanket on that hot black tar roof, while lathered up with baby oil and iodine to get a beautiful tan. I was nearly black every summer. Not Mern;

she didn't tan much and was usually as white as a ghost. We were chased down from that rooftop more than once. That was often because we were caught as we snuck up to the front edge of the building and looked down onto the State Road traffic.

Aunt Flo also taught us how to ice skate at the frozen tennis courts near her house in Brooklyn Heights. I recall once when Fran walked three blocks, all the way back to Aunt Flo's house, in Barbara's skates that Gert Fisher had given her. Fran and I loved Aunt Flo. The more we talked about her, the more our father badmouthed her. He said Aunt Flo didn't care about us because she never tried to visit while we were in the foster home.

I barely remember my grandparents. We didn't spend much time with either set of them, and they also never came to see us during the five years we were with the Fishers. My paternal grandparents were Anna Florence Manning Smith and Peter Smith. They lived in an impoverished part of Cleveland's east side. My father's dad, Arthur Bohner Sr., died before I ever met him. Grandpa Smith, his stepfather, was a very tall, thin man. He wore coveralls and a long-sleeved white shirt. Every time he saw me, he called me "Patty on the Railroad Tracks." He often sang an old Irish song called "Paddy on the Railway." It was a funny song that increased in speed with each verse. He liked to make us laugh. My Grandma Smith was very Irish with green eyes and fire red and grey hair. She was the tiniest woman I had ever seen with an abundance of energy. We were told she was like dynamite—small, but mighty. I really enjoyed her, but I believe I saw her less than ten times.

My maternal grandmother was Ruth Voss. We called her the "Holy Roller." She played church songs on her loud organ every time we visited her home. Grandma Voss always called us heathens. Her favorite song seemed to be "Bringing in the Sheep," which she sang in her screechy voice at the top of her lungs. We didn't learn until decades later that the song was actually called "Bringing in the Sheaves" and there were no sheep involved. Ruth Voss's second or third husband was Leonard Koller. I just remember he was blind and used a white cane to get around the house. He seemed like a nice guy.

CHAPTER 5

Hanging with Mern

A friend is a present you give to yourself.
~Robert Louis Stevenson~

Mern missed a great deal of school due to illness. One year she was quite sick with spinal meningitis and had to be quarantined. Mern had to repeat that half of the school year, so we were no longer in the same class. She loved to read, but never liked going to school. Mern quit school as soon as she was legally able to, at age 16. We still hung out together sometimes. Then she got married when she was only 18 or 19. Her husband, Steve, was a hard-working, great guy. And a very good daddy. Mern was bored and needed some excitement in her life. Sometimes I believe she got divorced just because I did. Unfortunately, Mern was married and divorced two more times after Steve.

As kids, Mern and I used to walk a lot. We often walked around the block and stopped in to visit Louise, "the Salt & Pepper Lady." Mern was so happy because Louise was her own middle name. She worked downtown and got off the bus at the end of our street, so we carried her bags home for her. Louise had a huge collection of salt and pepper shakers. One time she gave us each a set of our choice. Mine was a little dog and a cat. I don't remember Mern's. Another time, Louise gave us fresh roasted chestnuts and hot chocolate. We had never eaten chestnuts before. Louise was such a kind lady, no matter how tired she must have been from work, she always had time for us.

Once, on our walk around the block, we saw a naked guy standing in front of his screen door. After going by again and again to be certain, we went home and called the police. For much longer walks, we went to Gold Circle and Spartan-Atlantic Discount Stores. We liked to play with the puppies in cages. If we had any money from babysitting, we would spend it on clothes or bathroom supplies like toothpaste, shampoo, or lotion. Sometimes I bought cigarettes from a vending machine. I smoked back then, at age fifteen, because I thought it was cool. One time, while walking home from shopping, I burned the tip of Mern's nose with my cigarette. I didn't mean to do it. After she was over being mad, we laughed about it.

My father caught me smoking at home once. I heard him coming up the steps, so I blew smoke out the bedroom window and shoved the ashtray under my bed. He never acknowledged the cigarette, but just said, "It's your own damn health. Do what you want." I took that as permission to continue smoking. Funny—that was kind of the same response I got when I asked if I could have pierced ears back in seventh grade. He said, "Do whatever the hell you want." So, I did! I pierced them myself with ice cubes, a sewing needle, and rubbing alcohol. And they never once were infected!

We spent a great deal of time sitting on an old couch Mern's parents tossed out onto the porch. We sang a lot, talked, and did a great deal of people-watching. Mern and I loved when the old "Paper and Ragman" came down our street with a horse and cart. He was a gruff looking guy and had a very low, raspy voice. He cried out: "PA-PER RA-AGS!" He almost sang it and turned the word "rags" into at least two syllables. He was kind of the recycle man before his time. The paper ragman paid people for the materials they gave him, just a few cents here and there. Neighbors would run outside to his wagon when they heard him. That's when we jumped down off the porch to pet the aged, tired horse. The ragman accepted things like bundles of old newspapers and magazines, cloth, or rags, and kitchen items such as pots and pans, and threw them into his wagon. We asked why he did it and he said it was his job. He took all the stuff to the junkyard and made a little extra money from selling it there.

Mern and I talked about everything and just enjoyed the time being young. She always wanted to leave Cleveland and dreamed about living in Hollywood. She hoped to be famous one day. I shared my dreams with her, too. I wanted to go to college, become a teacher, and someday live on the water. We talked about boys and our futures. Mern wanted to marry young and get out of that house. I didn't want to get married for a very long time. I had to get my education first. Whenever we talked, if we said the same words at the exact same time, we punched each other in the arm and said, "You owe me a Coke!" We laughed every time we heard our next-door neighbors, Mr. and Mrs. Shearer, blow a loud, shrill whistle to get their five kids to come running. It was straight out of *The Sound of Music.* Those kids immediately stopped whatever they were doing and ran home as fast as they could. Mern and I tried to imagine what life was like, inside their house when nobody was looking.

It was a special treat when one of our parents came home on a Saturday with groceries. Then Mern or I would go in and beg for a piece of American cheese. The other person went in and got some Kool-aide for us to share. We each got half of that slice—always! Unless of course, if one of us stole a second slice. Did you know that one piece of cheese can yield 100 tiny bites? We each took our share and tore it into fifty little pieces. That made the cheese last much longer and we felt like we had more to eat. I fondly think of Mern every time I eat a slice of cheese. Maybe I'll break my next slice into 100 pieces just to honor my friend.

Another time, Mern and I were sitting out on our front porch. We both loved storms and were excited to see lightning and hear the loud cracks of thunder. Between the flashes and booms we would count seconds: "One Mississippi, two Mississippi, three Mississippi." You then had to divide the number of seconds by five to get the mileage. That would tell how many miles away the storm was located. I don't know how accurate it was, but we loved doing it. One stormy day, we were catching raindrops on our tongues by leaning over the porch rail. Suddenly, the rail gave out and we fell off the porch together, with Mern landing on me. She had the breath knocked out of her and couldn't talk. Her angry parents took her to the hospital. They wanted me to ride along and get checked out. My father, Frank Sr. said, "Don't get involved!" That's how he handled things.

Mern's father was another drunk—a very mean one. Each Friday was payday, and he would come home intoxicated and beat the crap out of his wife and kids. They literally had to go and sleep in the car every Friday night for as long as I can remember. It made no difference which season it was. He threw them out in the hot summer, freezing winter snowstorms, pouring rain—it didn't matter. But that never stopped Mern from pushing all the buttons to infuriate her father.

Once, the two of us went to a carnival. Mern met a cute carnival worker and wanted to stay. We were only about 15 years old. It was late and I knew I wanted to go home, so I left her there. Mern ended up staying with this guy talking all night, until sunrise.

The next thing I knew, someone was banging on my bedroom door that led up to the attic. Like our basement, the duplex shared a giant open attic space. Each side had their own steps and a door leading into a bedroom. So Mern's father caught her trying to sneak in at dawn. Mern ran out of her bedroom, up through the attic, and down the steps to my bedroom. Her father appeared right at the foot of my bed, in his striped pajama bottoms only, carrying a huge belt. And he had a giant beer belly, so that belt was big! Mern used our escape route to avoid that beating. She ran through my bedroom, to the bathroom, flung open the window, climbed out, and shimmied down the peach tree just in time. No way could that mean old man catch her. He was irate but didn't say a word to me. He just headed back up to the attic the same way he had come down through my room. Her dad was pure evil!

That man, Mike Grycan, changed his name to Grayson out of nowhere when we were kids. He came home one day and told Mern to spell her name from then on as Grayson, so she did. Like my father, Mern's father drove a truck for a living. He worked for a different company. I think he drove for Sterling Linder, the downtown department store that had that beautiful giant Christmas tree. It was the country's largest indoor Christmas tree at that time, standing at 60 feet tall. Mike's side job was a bookie, where he ran bets for the illegal Numbers game. That's before the State Lottery Commissions made playing numbers okay. Apparently, bookies had a lot of enemies. Gamblers, losers, and the IRS agents were among them. We weren't sure which of those caused the sudden name change.

Long after we had all moved away from the duplex, Mern's dad, Mike Grycan, or Grayson, or whomever, won one of the biggest jackpots in the Ohio Lottery. Early on, 1.3 million was unheard of. You can imagine what that kind of money did to a family like his. All I know is, none of his family members were talking to each other at his funeral. Money reared its ugly head! Also, before his death, he made the news again when he was arrested for shoplifting. The family claimed he was senile, put the item in his pocket, then forgot to take it out at the register. But that wasn't the story. Of course, the news was "Parma Millionaire Lottery Winner Gets Caught Shoplifting!" How ironic Mern and I were living in a duplex and both of our fathers were truck driving, no-good drunks.

Chapter 6

Who Was My Father?

Although the world is full of pain, it is also full of overcoming it.
~Helen Keller~

"My Father." How do I write that phrase sarcastically?

There is no doubt that moving to Cleveland to live with our father was an unfortunate mistake. No one ever asked for input from us kids. We were not at all prepared for this life-changing move. It was handled rather matter-of-factly. Basically, we were just told, "You three are going to live with your father next Saturday." At the time, we thought that was the best news ever! It didn't take long for us to see the reality of the situation. We clearly had been holding onto a fantasy regarding our father rescuing us from the foster home. Fantasy and reality are worlds apart.

While living with our father, I hated birthdays and most holidays. He was always sloshed! No more great birthday parties like Aunt Gert used to throw for us. My favorite holiday was Halloween! It had nothing to do with our father. We did it all on our own. We made costumes for ourselves. Usually that meant we were baseball players because we had mitts and hats. Or we were bums because all we needed was to smear burnt cork on our faces and wear raggedy clothes. Back then we trick-or-treated two nights, Beggar's Night and then on Halloween again. We covered different streets each evening and people were so generous! We would hustle and collect a full grocery-sized paper bag both nights! We had so much candy we swam in it!

My worst holiday was definitely Christmas. Every Christmas Eve our father held big poker games at our house. We had to hide out in our bedrooms the entire night. They smoked, drank, and played all night long until near daylight! On Christmas morning, us kids went downstairs to open the presents we had purchased and wrapped for our own selves. That's how we did Christmas. Our father gave us a little money and then we walked all the way to Giant Tiger's on Brookpark and Pearl Road; three miles round trip. We picked out some things, usually clothes and a baseball for ourselves, and rushed home to wrap them.

We also walked up a few blocks to the Produce Market on State Road. There we purchased a Christmas tree and dragged it all the way home for decorating. Getting the tree to stand up was definitely a problem. Usually, us kids tied it to a door and a window or something. We made paper chains and any type of decorations we could come up with to make the bare tree look better. Somehow, we never failed to have silver tinsel. Our father didn't do anything to help, or to make Christmas better for us. I honestly don't have one good holiday memory while living with him. Even now, I still have a great deal of negative feelings around Christmas.

I hated my father and was thoroughly embarrassed by him. Everyone recognized the drunkard in the bar window. When our father wasn't working, he was drunk. He looked and acted like Jackie Gleason, constantly drinking and smoking his unfiltered Lucky Strikes. His nickname was "Buck," but I don't know why. My father was a Teamster and drove a semi-truck for Lyons Transportation Lines. The motto on the semi bumpers was "Here Today, There Tomorrow." I remember wishing my father was "there," wherever that was, instead of home. I liked it best when our father ran his truck loads out of town for a few days at a time. He was highly active in the Teamsters Local 407; he even became a union steward at one time.

One day, our father, Frank Sr., was involved in an accident while working. His semi was sandwiched between two other trucks. Neck and back injuries led to his never working again. Frank Sr. felt like the Teamsters turned their backs on him once he was no longer driving a truck. He decided to sue the trucking company. Several years later, after I had already left home, he used his lawsuit earnings to buy a bar, Hillcrest Tavern, which later became Wexlers. Just what Frank Bohner needed in his life—a bar!

Somehow, while driving a truck, my father was connected to some of the big guys in the Teamsters. It wasn't unusual for one of us kids to answer the phone and hear that it was some union guy like Bill or Jackie Presser, Babe Triscaro, Allen Friedman, Tommy Lee, John Tanski, or Tiny Moore. A lot of times we had to lie and say he wasn't there. Even Jimmy Hoffa called twice that I recall when I was in high school.

My father idolized Hoffa; or at least he publicly did. On a few occasions when he was in the hospital after his trucking accident, my father hung Hoffa's personally autographed picture above his bed, covering up a cross or a picture of Jesus. That usually got the doctors and nurses talking. Hoffa sent all of us kids large black and white glossy pictures with real signatures. I threw mine out, but I think Fran still has hers. Jimmy Hoffa also sent us beautiful silver watches with safety chains, that had his face etched on the back. Mine was stolen when I worked at a summer camp. Jackie Presser gave Fran and me circle pins for one Christmas. Somehow, I held on to that pin.

After a while, my father began taping phone conversations with those union officials on a little cassette player. I still have one of those tapes of a conversation between my father and Tiny Moore. We later wondered if there was any connection between those recordings and our Godfather, the FBI Agent, whom we never saw again. I don't really know what our father was up to, but I do know that he was constantly worried about something. Frank Sr. kept a loaded handgun under a pillow on the chair where he watched TV. He also kept it in bed when he slept. That was pretty scary! The man never explained the gun to us. Luckily, he never had to use it.

CHAPTER 7

A Daughter's Nightmare

That which does not kill us makes us stronger.
~Friedrich Nietzsche~

There were two items in my father's bedroom closet that scared me; yet they also made me curious. One was a prosthetic leg wrapped in a white chenille bedspread. My father's friend, Ray, lost a teenage son to bone cancer. The prosthesis had belonged to the son. I have absolutely no idea why it was in our house, but as a ten-year old, that leg really frightened me!

The other item in that same closet was my father's army rifle from the Korean War. He was a Military Police Officer; even received a Purple Heart. He claimed he had a piece of metal in his head. I am ashamed to admit this out loud, but I used to go upstairs to his bedroom and take that rifle out from under the blanket in the corner of the closet. Then I would cock it and aim it at that bar window where he sat, across the street. We had sheer white curtains and I was smart enough to make sure I couldn't be seen, while I pulled the trigger repeatedly. Thank goodness that rifle was never loaded, or this would have been a whole different story. And I didn't do it just one time. I did it often when I was mad at him or thought about how much I really hated him.

I had good reason to hate my father. He sexually molested me, his own daughter! He would often come home drunk very late at night. He'd pull me out of bed and take me downstairs or even to my little brother's room,

43

where Frank Jr. slept on the top bunk. Looking back, there were obviously problems with the marriage because Ronnie, who was ten or eleven years old, slept with his mother, while my father slept on the bottom bunk in the boys room.

I always wondered why Fran never woke up, or said anything, when our drunken father pulled me out of bed. Her bed was so close to mine. Maybe she was afraid, or maybe she didn't wake up. I should have yelled. Why didn't I scream? I guess I didn't scream because I didn't believe that anyone would help me.

I won't go into detail, but my father did and said things no father should ever do, or say to a child, especially his own daughter. I still sometimes wake up crying, or in a sweat, because I am scared that my father will be home any minute. I don't imagine those nightmares will ever go away. Perhaps the worst thing my father ever said to me was, "If you tell anyone you will have to go back to the foster home. They will put me in jail." I only wish I knew what a positive solution that would have been. You must realize, that was during a time when no one ever talked about such a thing. I didn't tell one soul until many, many years later.

One time, our stepmother unexpectedly walked into the boys' bedroom as my father had me in that bed. She peeked in, looked right at us, and went back to bed! She didn't say one word—not then, not ever! She never offered to help me or anything. Never did she speak about it. I hated her for that! All I know is that she stayed for about three more years until she took her son and left. We finally got rid of Kay and Ronnie. Frank Sr. and Kay were divorced when I was fourteen. Then I had to do all the cooking, washing, cleaning, shopping, and everything. I don't know why, but Fran and Frank did almost nothing to help with the housework.

Around the time my stepmother left, I recall Linda, a classmate, saying to me, "You always seem so happy. Doesn't it ever bother you that you don't have a mother?" I told her that I had adopted a coping technique long ago, that I called "Faking myself out." Somehow, when my life was tough, I was able to live within the moment and just focus on something fun. I was very good at avoiding emotional pain. To survive, I pretended or convinced myself that it didn't exist. That's what carried me through a great many unpleasant events in my life.

My father often secretly asked me if I remembered anything from the night before. Of course, I remembered, but I always played dumb. That was another one of my defenses. Pretend nothing happened and you will get through this. Now, all these years later, I know I should have told my teacher or someone I trusted. I didn't; I just held it inside for too many years. It was too evil to discuss with anyone. I thought it was my fault. I didn't want my father to go to jail. I didn't want to go to another foster home. You know, all the classic reasons for not telling. I remember going to school and just looking around the classroom at each female, thinking, "I wonder if her father does that to her." I even picked out which girls I thought it probably happened to. For years, I kept planning a way to get out of that world. And meanwhile, I just lived day-to-day, creating my own happiness.

CHAPTER 8

School Was My Refuge

Education is the most powerful weapon
which you can use to change the world.
~Nelson Mandela~

I have always liked learning. That's one reason school meant something very special to me. But I also knew that whenever I was at school, I was free from all drama and evil at home. I was safe! I could get a great deal of positive attention from the adults when I performed well in class. Well, all except for handwriting, that is. Often, I would have all A's on my report card, but a B in handwriting. That B was a generous gift from my teacher. My cursive handwriting skills never did seem to improve. In all other subjects, I listened to everything that was being taught and learned easily. Even homework was enjoyable to me. School was fun and a very safe place. My teachers always made me feel supported and encouraged. Since third grade, I thought that teaching was likely going to be my chosen profession. By fourth grade I was certain, and never changed that goal.

One time, also in third grade, my report card was very good until I turned it over to the "Teacher Comments" section. Somehow nothing else mattered to me. I really wanted my teacher to like me. She wrote: "Patty needs to improve upon her personal appearance." I was absolutely crushed by that comment. We had so few clothes to wear. My sister and I washed things out in the sink and tried to dry them for the next day.

White socks just never remained white. We didn't iron our clothes and had messy hair. The worst part was that my father used to pick up shoes for us. I'm not sure where he got them, but they were awful! It looked like I was wearing old lady pumps in the third grade! I could hardly walk in those things! We had wrinkled blouses, ill-fitting skirts, thick white bobby socks, and pumps that didn't fit our feet. The teacher was, no doubt, justified in her tactless comment.

Unfortunately, during that particular year, we also had bedbugs in our home. They bit us at night, leaving sores and blood streaks everywhere. My skin was a mess. The teacher was right; I did need to improve my appearance, but it wasn't because I was negligent. No adult in the house gave a crap. I remember being so hurt by that remark. From then on, I always checked the teacher's comments before I looked at any grades. The fact that I still recall what she said shows how much power a teacher's words can have when a child is so vulnerable. I didn't like that teacher anymore and knew I wanted to be a better teacher.

One other negative memory I have of elementary school occurred twice a year for what seemed like forever. All through grade school we had to make cute little cards and projects for "Mother's Day and Father's Day." You can imagine how awful that was for a kid like me, or for a child who lost a parent through death. It was a constant reminder of what we didn't experience that most other kids seemed to have. I usually pretended to enjoy the activity and then throw my project in the trash can on the way out. I really hated those projects.

I was a responsible student and I enjoyed being in classroom presentations on stage. One time in fifth grade, our assembly was about educational learning tools. I decorated a huge cardboard box with blue paper, to look like a Webster's Dictionary. My teacher brought in a graduation cap with a tassel for my head. I wore this giant box with holes for my neck and arms while explaining the purpose of a dictionary. That was a particularly proud elementary school moment for me.

Another activity I loved about elementary school was the gardening program. In the summer, we could buy seed packets for home planting and we could sign up to have a plot of land at Benjamin Franklin School. Everyone loved those Benji gardens! We were taught how to tend the soil, plant the seeds, water, and weed. Then we harvested huge crops, if we had taken good care of our garden. Every week we went home with a giant basket of fresh vegetables. It was awesome!

During my last year in elementary school I had two jobs. One, I was paid fifty cents per week to perform. I had to pick up a little kindergarten boy daily and take him safely to school. He lived just a block away, so it was convenient and such an easy task.

The other assignment I held was my favorite. I was the Captain of the School Safety Patrol. My white sash had a special gold badge because I had the highest rank. My job was to schedule and assign all patrols to specific times and positions. Then I had to monitor the patrols and report back to the teacher-in-charge. The teacher who selected me to the position had been my fifth-grade teacher. She was my favorite teacher ever. Mrs. Oschek usually pulled my ponytail whenever she caught me drinking at the fountain and then she'd wink or laugh. She loved teasing me. I still remember the exact seat I was in when I asked Mrs. Oschek the difference in "probly" and "probably." I was stunned when she said the first one wasn't a real word! She also taught me the comparison of good, better, and best through a little rhyme: "Good, better, best. Never let it rest, until your good is better, and until your better is best." Those are just two of the fun facts I recall from her classroom. Mrs. Oschek was an excellent teacher and taught me a great deal. As the patrol captain, I made sure I reported to her personally each morning, even though I was no longer in her class.

During the summer months, Mrs. Oschek picked me up and took me out to her family home numerous times.

It was a sweet lifetime bonus when I ran into her decades later. We were colleagues at the Martha Jennings Scholar Lectures. My favorite teacher was absolutely thrilled to see that I had become a classroom teacher and that I was being acknowledged for excellence in my profession. I was able to let her know that she had been such a positive role-model for me so long ago. She had lit the fire under my career choice, without even knowing it. I was so happy to finally have the opportunity to tell Mrs. Oschek how important she had been in my life.

In sixth grade, I was in a play for our promotion celebration. Because I was the Safety Patrol Captain, I felt honored to lead the Color Guard. We carried a large American flag into the auditorium where I led the student body in The Pledge of Allegiance. Then I had to explain the shapes and colors of the United States flag and what they represented. Lastly, we showed the students how to properly fold, carry, and store the flag. I loved getting up on that stage.

The only assembly I disliked was an orchestra concert back in fourth grade. I had just started taking violin lessons at school. In just a few short weeks we had to play "Mary Had a Little Lamb" and "Go tell Aunt Rhody." I did fine with the first one. Strangely, I still know the finger positions. 2-1-0-1-2-2-2, 1-1-1, 2-2-2, 2-1-0-1-2-2-2-2, 1-1-2-1-0. Why in the world would I continue to remember that? I guess I still recall those positions because they clearly match the well-known song. The second song was a different story, and I was terrified of it. The song sounded like a funeral march to me. It was actually about an old goose who died. I had to fake it on stage in front of the whole school. I just knew everyone could tell I had no idea what I was doing. I was so embarrassed that I quit violin class the next day.

My stepmother came to the school for parent conferences, assemblies, and my promotion ceremony. The only time our father set foot in any of our schools was for Sabin Oral Sunday. On three consecutive Sundays in the early 1960's people went en masse to churches and schools to receive a sugar cube or a spoonful of liquid. They contained a vaccine to fight against the polio outbreaks. Other than that, our father never came to our schools. We couldn't understand why he seemed to care so little about education. He just bragged about the good grades we received; especially when we were rewarded at school with tickets to the Cleveland Indians games. When we asked about his schooling, we never got straight answers. He simply told us that he went to "The School of Hard Knocks" or to "Reform School" and he said that was all we needed to know. We never learned much truth about any of his life. Somewhere in his army records, I recently read that he had two years of high school credit. What is absolutely astonishing to me is that despite such a dysfunctional family, at least six, maybe seven, of my mother's eight children had some college education. I don't know about Little May. And at least half of them received one degree, while others completed multiple degrees. I find that rather amazing. Each of us must have found positive role models somewhere in our developmental years.

CHAPTER 9

My Sister, Fran

Sisters from similar seeds can produce very different gardens.
~Patty Wyman~

I must give my sister, Fran, partial credit for my desire to learn. Fran was three years ahead of me in school and was the epitome of a great student. She took school seriously and always achieved at a very high level. Fran is brilliant and completed two college degrees. At Case Western Reserve she received a degree in Art History. In Toronto she received a second degree in Interior Decorating and Design.

When we were very young, Fran took us to the library once a week. We loved checking out books and couldn't get enough to read. One of the first chapter books I recall reading was *The Bobbsey Twins in Mystery Cave*. I remember being obsessed with mysteries from about fourth grade on. I still love a good mystery, just as I still love learning. Fran was more of an introvert and spent most of her time with books. I, on the other hand, was the extrovert of the family. I was out on the streets hanging with my friends, while Fran was home studying. She is extremely bright and retains just about everything. That's why she is so great when she plays *Jeopardy*, or any other trivia game. I always wanted her to compete on the *Jeopardy Show*. I still do!

Fran and I weren't always nice to each other. We shared a bedroom for many years with twin beds that were just two to three feet apart. I sometimes talked in my sleep. Fran has since admitted tormenting me at night. She was especially evil during our bedbug period. She threw tiny Kleenex wads at me to make me think the bugs, or rats, were going to bite me. I'm sure it was fun for her. Not so fun for me though. Fran and I were very different and fought all the time. Drawing a line down the center of the room was not uncommon for us. The problem was I had to walk on her side to get out of the bedroom. Once, the fight was violent. I have no idea what it was about, but she ended up throwing a pair of scissors all the way across the room at me. They found a resting place in my thigh. Lots of screaming and plenty of blood! Our father yelled upstairs, and Fran begged me not to say anything. I didn't because I liked her more than I liked our father.

I wasn't always nice to Fran either. I remember one horrible time when we got a new puppy. Fran was in high school, and I was in junior high. She was mad because she had to take the puppy out in the freezing cold. I was glad Fran got picked and I didn't. She grabbed my coat off the hook and I told her she couldn't use it, but she took it anyway. I slammed the door after her. Unfortunately, Fran's arm got caught in the door. She quickly pulled it back straight through the glass plated window. I remember getting yelled at because in a panic, I tried to stop the bleeding with dirty dish towels. Fran's wrist was seriously slashed and she had to be rushed to the ER. The plastic surgeon was called in and commented about how close she was to severing an artery in her wrist. I think my sister still has a big scar and permanent nerve damage from that incident. I just know that by the time I went to high school I already had a reputation amongst the teachers who liked Fran. And let's just say it wasn't good. I recall the German teacher saying, "Oh, you're the one who threw your sister through the window." That's not exactly how it happened, but that was her take on the story.

Our father tried to sue the landlord, Mr. Albert Fink, for Fran's injury. We always thought of that landlord when Ghoulardi was on TV talking about the rat finks in Cleveland and Parma. I don't know if our father ever won that lawsuit.

CHAPTER 10

Making Our Own Entertainment

Nostalgia is a file that removes the rough edges
from the good old days.
~Doug Larsen~

We really didn't watch much television, but we did enjoy a few regular shows. *The Three Stooges*, *The Twilight Zone*, *The Fugitive*, and *Bonanza* were among them. Our favorite show, by far, was the *Ghoulardi* show on Friday nights. Ghoulardi was a fictional character from Cleveland, who hosted weekly science fiction or horror shows. His shock theater was a huge hit, especially among impressionable teens. To me, Ghoulardi was kind of like the television version of *Mad Magazine's*, Alfred E. Neuman. He was always in costume with trick glasses, a long goatee, and horns in his hair. Ghoulardi was into unusual things like polka music, firecrackers, anti-authoritarian attitudes, and satires on cities like Parma. He relentlessly teased about white socks, pink Flamingos, finks, rat finks, or k-nifs, as he called them. Viewers anticipated the exact moments when Ghoulardi would interrupt the exciting part of the rather poor movies through visual effects. The blue screen image allowed a very tiny version of him to run through the movies as though he was being chased by the monsters. He loved to use fun words in his comedy routines. Ghoulardi told viewers to remember to drink their "ghoul-aide," and work hard to become "magna ghoul laudes."

We lived in the first house right next to Cypress Beverage. The beverage store is still there today, but our old house was razed years ago. For a while, we received an allowance of fifty cents a week on Saturdays, following paydays. Immediately, us kids would rush over to the beverage store and buy a bottle of pop and some penny candy, or baseball cards. The owner, Stosh, liked us and often threw in a few extras, like a stick pretzel, a piece of bubble gum, or a baseball card or two that came from an open pack. He was good to us. Sometimes we went across State Road to a store called Producers Dairy. They had the best ice cream cones! Saving money just wasn't an option for us kids back then.

Kitty-cornered from our house, across Cypress, was the State Road Tavern. How convenient! Our father could sit right there all day on the bar stool in the big fat picture window. That's how he "watched" his kids. We were never allowed inside the bar, but that didn't stop Mern and me from watching everything that went on over there. For many, many years we hung out on our huge front porch where the lushes constantly filtered in and out of the bar. We witnessed numerous fights between barflies, late night wasted pukers, and couples making out in the parking lot in their cars. We loved when the cops came and cleared everyone out. Late at night, just as the boozers were getting wild, the entire sky turned red and orange when the steel mills in the distant Flats stoked up their chimney fires.

Right across from our porch lived Dave. We called him Davey Crockett, the Deer Hunter because he loved to hunt. Dave would bring deer home, tied to the top of his old brown station wagon. Then he'd hang the deer in his yard and skin it. It was gross, but for some reason we always watched. Ironically, many years later, Mern had a walk-on part in a movie called *The Deer Hunter,* starring Robert De Niro. In her scene she was shopping in a grocery store with Meryl Streep. Mern got the part by bringing an old car to the movie set they were filming in Cleveland. She had borrowed my silver Volvo, so it was also in the movie. Mern wanted to be a movie star. She claimed that her mother named her after Marilyn Monroe. I guess that's why she bleached her hair bright blonde for at least fifty-five years.

Mern and I loved animals. We each had dogs and sometimes cats. My brother had a dime store turtle, but it walked away one day. We suspected that it may have crawled down the basement drain. Mern's family dog was Rusty. He was the most beautiful dog I had ever seen. Rusty was a huge collie with very long soft, flowing hair. We loved brushing that fur. Rusty was always calm and majestic. My dog, Jasper, was from a cage at the Spartan-Atlantic Store. He was a brown and black mutt and I absolutely loved him. We picked up stray cats more than once and brought them home. One cat, my father said I could keep, had to sleep in the basement. The very next morning we heard squealing coming up the basement steps. That cat had eight babies overnight! When they were big enough, I had to give all of them away, including the mother cat.

The only thing us kids loved about the bar where my father spent all his free time, was their hamburgers. Often on Friday night, when the *Ghoulardi* show was on television, our father would run home, or usually he sent someone else, with hot hamburgers for us kids. We had never been to any fast-food places, so this was a very special treat. He normally stayed at the bar until closing so we would already be in bed by the time he came home. If we heard him open the outer door, we ran up to bed so we wouldn't have to see him.

Water was always a major positive part of our lives. We taught ourselves to swim early on. During the summer months, nearly every single day, we walked to Loew Pool on Oak Park. We practically lived at the pool and were there from opening until closing. The pool shut down for one hour each day for a dinner break, at which time we hiked around the fence to the fruit trees in the back. We climbed the trees and filled up on crabapples, plums, and pears. That was dinner every day. It was especially great fun to see who had half a worm sticking out of their fruit.

Loew Pool closed one day a week for cleaning. That's when we drove our bikes down to Brookside Pool at the zoo. We loved that big old concrete swimming circle. It had a huge flat platform with ladders in the center. We didn't all have bikes, so we had to double up and ride with the kids who owned one. We did some crazy things like riding up and down Snake Hill on someone's handlebars. Other times we held on to the driver's shoulders and stood with our feet on the nuts and bolts on the back tire axle. Snake Hill was a very steep, winding brick road that led right out onto busy Brookside Road near the zoo entrance. We would go up and down that hill, screaming for pure entertainment. Sometimes, I can't believe we survived half the things we did back then.

There were no other girls to play with in our neighborhood, so I hung out with Mern and the Ryan boys every day. The Ryans were part of a huge family with something like twelve kids. Their parents were probably very happy that their kids hung out all day with us. In the mornings, we usually played baseball in our big grassy yard, which was really a dust bowl, or in the Producers parking lot across the street. All the neighborhood kids came to play. We divided into teams for full games. We also liked to play 500 where you had to catch the ball for various amounts of points. The thrower tossed the ball to the catchers and called out how many points the catch would be worth. The player who got exactly 500 first became the next thrower. Sometimes we awkwardly tossed our own ball up and batted it out to the catchers, but that was a lot tougher.

Homerun Derby was another game we played, based on the old TV series. We all thought we were the best baseball players in the world. We watched a great deal of baseball back then. A lot of us neighborhood kids took busses downtown to see the Cleveland Indians play in the old Municipal Stadium. That was the coolest stadium ever! It seated more than 75,000 people for baseball and football games. That stadium had the best old wooden seats that the fans notoriously banged up and down to make the visiting teams nervous. Some very famous people held live concerts at the Municipal Stadium. Among them were Rod Stewart, The Rolling Stones, Bruce Springsteen, Michael Jackson, and the Beatles, to name a few.

As a teamster, my father received free box seat tickets for us. I remember long ago when we were able to sit right on the roof of the Indians' dugout. We talked to all the players like we knew them. We also loved to run in the very top row from one end to the other of the gigantic horseshoe-shaped structure. But we had the most fun in the bleachers. Unfortunately, many years later, that awesome stadium was literally shoved into Lake Erie in the name of progress. Separate, smaller facilities were built for the two different sports. However, they were never able to reconstruct the character and spirit of that old stadium. After the games, we sometimes swam in the dirty fountain on Mall C, downtown, before we got back on the bus to go home. We didn't really have to answer to anyone. Our father never cared about where we were or what time we got home. He usually wasn't there, so it didn't matter.

Late at night us kids would gamble for baseball cards instead of money. Poker, blackjack, seven card stud, and rummy were our favorite games. We imitated the adults we had seen by drinking ginger ale out of shot glasses. Of course, we had to have the candy cigarettes and the bubble gum cigars to make it more authentic looking.

Everyone kept their baseball cards in large paper bags or shoe boxes. None of us catalogued them into binders; we kept them fluid. When we got tired of the cards, we would hold a big Trade Day, or even more exciting was the Scramble Day. That's where we would toss all our cards into the air and scream "SCRAMBLE!" We liked to do it on windy days when the cards would go flying in all different directions. Of course, no one wanted to part with cards like Mickey Mantle, Ty Cobb, Minnie Minoso, Rocky Colavito, Joe DiMaggio, Ted Williams, or Stan Musial. Someone even had a Babe Ruth card, but it wasn't me. Everyone who wanted more cards would bring a paper bag and scramble to pick up as many as possible. Sometimes we would hide them up in the trees in the little wooded area or in the gulley in our backyard and kids would hunt for them.

That's the same gulley that had a big drain pole coming off the business building next to our yard. Once, I was so thirsty from playing out in the snow, I licked the ice on the pole. Yep! My tongue, sure enough, stuck to that ice just the way it happened to Ralphie in *A Christmas Story*. Wish I had seen the movie first and I would have known better. Meanwhile, Mern was no help. She just about wet her pants laughing so hard at my misfortune. But she did run home and get a cup of warm water to set me free.

We also played a card toss game, kind of like pitching pennies. We lined up and pitched a single baseball card against a brick wall when it was our turn. Whoever had the closest card to the wall won each round. If someone tossed a card and leaned it against the wall, they won. That move could only be outranked if someone else knocked it down in that same round. Once our cards were lost in various games, or given away in scrambles, we'd start collecting them all over again. We didn't have money, so baseball cards were a very valuable commodity to us kids. Over time, I hid my cards down in the basement on a window ledge. I really regretted not taking those baseball cards when I permanently left home.

We loved going to the movies. On Saturdays we walked to the Broadview Theater where we saw all the *Tarzan*, *Sinbad*, and *Tammy* movies you could ever imagine, for only twenty-five or fifty cents. Sharing tiny Jujubes went a long way. They were so chewy and got stuck in your teeth forever! After the show, we went next door to the Royal Castle. We shared mini burgers and birch beers. Then Mern would call home. She was careful to use the code: Ring twice and hang up so you get your dime back. Her mom would hear the two rings, but not pick up. She just came to pick us up right away. We cheated the phone company out of a lot of dimes. So did many other people.

Mern's mom was nice. As much as she loved her kids, she was terrified of her husband. I don't know that I ever saw her angry. She worked hard as a waitress in the German Club right by our house. Idell Grycan was illiterate; she just never had the opportunity to learn to read. She would shyly ask, "What does this say? I forgot my glasses." I remember once their old stove was replaced. She kept asking me what the buttons said. When I became a teacher, it was one of my life goals to teach Mern's mom to read. Regretfully, it never happened. Her husband forbade it and said, "She doesn't need to know that shit!" He liked to keep her ignorant; unaware of what was going on in the world. That made her more dependent upon him so she would never leave or throw his butt to the curb. Mern's mom died never having read a newspaper, a book, or a sentimental card her kids made for her. I just cannot even imagine living in a world like that!

CHAPTER 11

My Teen Years

Each friend represents a world in us,
a world possibly not born until they arrive,
and it is only by this meeting that a new world is born.
~Anais Nin~

By the time I was twelve years old I started hanging out at Dawning playground. During the summer months I was invited by the coach, Carol Krailo, to play softball for Dawning. I started to spend a great deal of time there and found I really loved being around Carol and those activities. I was the pitcher on the team and was obsessed with the sport. We played games against other playgrounds in the evenings. I had to have two pieces of Double Bubble Gum to calm my nerves whenever I pitched. I never had to worry if I forgot mine because the whole team knew my ritual and brought some gum, just in case. Playing baseball all those years in our backyard really paid off.

During the schoolyear, our playground coach, Carol, and her Christmas Day twin sister, Holly, went off to college at Ohio Wesleyan. I was thrilled because she wrote to me regularly and tried to keep me out of trouble. Meanwhile, I thought I was pretty cool because I belonged to the "Dawning Gang." Most of the time we behaved; playing baseball, four corners, kickball, dodgeball, jump rope, and dice. Sometimes we walked up to Our Lady of Good Counsel's playground. Our 'tough gang" just couldn't get enough of that crazy spinning merry-go-round. The King of the Mountain was the last one sitting on the raised dome at the center of the ride, where there was nothing to grasp onto. People ran around the ride, holding on, and pushing it so fast they fell down. Nothing made us dizzier, and nothing made us laugh more. We loved that thing!

Tagging with graffiti wasn't popular back then, but I did etch my name "Pat the Pro" everywhere I could. Once my sister saw it on a corner mailbox. She asked, "Why would you write that? Do you even know what that means? Pro is short for prostitute." She went on to define prostitute and I never wrote that again! Her lie worked!

Our gang members only got into trouble when we were treated unfairly. The manager at the drug store thought we were stealing from him, but we weren't. He let us come in just one-at-a-time. We argued and tried to make him understand we were innocent. Then he banned us from his store. I am ashamed to admit we retaliated by throwing rocks through his big picture window—more than once! Our gang members were fast and we loved when the cops chased us. We had our own squad car that normally answered calls to our Old Brooklyn Cleveland area. A lookout was assigned to watch for our number on that particular black and white with the cherry on top. The cops were decent to us though. They just asked us to calm down and leave the guy alone. We eventually did.

We found other mischief to get into, like hanging out in the Brooklyn Heights Cemetery. There, we sat around tombstones and told scary stories. Sometimes we'd hang-drop down into the mausoleum from the roof and hide in there. We were never into smoking or drinking, and certainly not into drugs at that time. Gangs really were just kids hanging out together. But we did protect our "turf." Once, I fought a girl I didn't even know because she tried to come onto our playground without permission. Talk about bullying! Hey! I never said this book was all about my proudest moments.

Of course, now I realize that having the cops chase us was an exciting, but stupid game. About three years later, my very first boyfriend from fourth grade, Danny Capp, was shot in the back and killed by a police officer when he was sixteen. He had stolen a car and was running from the law. As he tried to climb a fence, they shot him! I had not been hanging out with Danny and his brother, Michael, by that time. I saw it on the news and was devastated. Many years earlier, in fourth grade, our teacher quit after just two months. We weren't even a bad class. Cleveland Schools had a severe teacher and classroom shortage in 1960. Students were divided into half-day sessions to report to school. Our group reported in the afternoon. So, in the mornings I would hang out at Danny's house. I don't recall his parents ever being home. He taught me to make grilled cheese sandwiches and scrambled eggs. Danny was kind of a "bad boy" and often got into trouble at school. But I remember him as someone who had beautiful platinum blonde hair hanging down to his eyes and a smile that could win anybody over.

We were normal kids who did some very dumb things. I remember when I was twelve and my junior high school, Charles A. Mooney, was under construction. The Dawning Gang walked up there every day to check on the progress. I shudder now when I think of how we used to walk the naked I-beams on the second and third stories, just for something to do. No walls, no floors—just metal frames that outlined the building's floors and rooms. I can't even imagine my kids or grandkids doing something that stupid! We must have been very lucky!

Dave "Rath" was my boyfriend in the Dawning Gang when I was thirteen. He was my first real boyfriend. I remember the very instant he grabbed my hand when we were all darting across the main road, as cars headed right toward us. Suddenly we were boyfriend and girlfriend. He was a very cute guy with longish dark wavy hair that he slicked back.

He dressed like the typical "Greaser" in sharkskin, iridescent clothes, and the banlon collared shirt with a leather jacket. Of course, he reeked of Brut, Canoe, or English Leather that he bathed in daily. When he transferred from a Catholic school to our junior high the whole school was abuzz with talk of that cute new kid! No one could believe he was my boyfriend until he met me by my locker at the end of the day. Soon after he joined our school, some rumor was going around about how people had seen him downtown, dressed in bellbottoms and hanging out with the hippies. At that time, there were no hippies living in our neighborhood. I confronted him and he admitted that he liked both sets of friends. I was okay with that. But I never did get to see him dressed like a hippie. He dumped me on New Year's Eve, and I was crushed!

Our junior high school was completed when I was in the middle of seventh grade. There was something special about having the opportunity to go to a brand-new school. Suddenly we had woodshops, home economics rooms, a giant cafeteria, beautiful well-lit classrooms, a great auditorium, and a huge gym. We even had a planetarium in our school. One of the coolest parts about opening a new school was that we had the chance to do all the "firsts." We democratically selected the school colors, named the sports teams, chose the mascot, voted on the school song, and so on. The Mooney Mustangs wore red and white. We felt like it was really our school.

Junior high at Mooney, where I met some lifelong friends, was so much fun. Sixty years later, several of us are still very close. Friends have always been my surrogate family and mean everything to me. Two of my closest friends from way back then are Chris and Sandy. We have been through so much together. Graduations, weddings, divorces, births, grandkids, deaths, and so much more have all made us like family. We were in adult bowling and golf leagues together. Chris, Sandy, and I are very different, but we honestly have never had an argument or spoken unkind words to each other during all these years. Teddi is another friend from that junior high crowd. She ended up going to college with me for a while. We are sincerely friends who love each other and are able to respect our differences.

At Mooney Junior High, most of my friends and I shared some classes where we got into trouble more than once. Our favorite escapade was when some of us were in a home economics sewing class. The class was rather boring because making an apron is only fun for about one minute. All those great adolescent brains working together were able to concoct some instant excitement! We took Sandy's tomato-shaped pincushion and decorated it like something from outer space. Her pincushion was the messiest one in the class! It had needles and funny pins sticking out, with varied lengths of brightly colored ribbon and tangled wads of thread hanging down from it. After adding more threads and ribbon of many colors and lengths, we attached a very long piece of ribbon and stuck a note to it that said, "Hi! I am visiting from Mars!" *My Favorite Martian* was a very popular TV series at the time. Anyhow, our little group sat on the windowsill and opened the classroom window. We knew the cafeteria was below us and that it was study hall time. Very slowly the pincushion UFO was lowered down until we heard a lot of laughter. We bobbed it up and down several times before quickly pulling it back up and inside the window. It was easy to pretend like nothing happened, until there was a knock at the door. A note was delivered to the teacher that Sandy received a detention for her little prank. Of course, we never stopped to realize that Sandy's pincushion had her name on the bottom of it! Each of us confessed and received detentions together because we couldn't let Sandy take all the blame. Hearing that laughter from a whole study hall full of kids was worth one after-school detention.

Also, in junior high, we were all in English class together. Each of us had nicknames from the TV show, *The Little Rascals*. I was Spanky. Sandy's nickname was Cotton and Chris was Alfalfa. Every time Sandy went up front to give a book report, we would rub our heads or pat our bellies and mouth the words "I wish Cotton was a monkey." That was a line from one of our favorite *Little Rascals* episodes. Poor Sandy could never speak in front of the class without cracking up. Unfortunately, I feel a little guilty because Sandy's English grade was likely impacted by our actions.

Half of our lunch period was free time. Students could go to a Gab Room, where we could just talk to our friends. We could help a teacher, go to tutoring, or watch part of a movie for less than fifteen minutes each day. Without a doubt, the one movie that really freaked us out was Alfred Hitchcock's, *The Birds!* That was the scariest movie we had ever seen up to that point in our young lives. Our group couldn't wait to finish eating so we could get front row seats each day. When you only see a movie for fifteen minutes a day it takes nearly two weeks to watch. The suspense held our attention when we had to wait for the weekends to pass before we could see what happened next. We loved that movie because it scared the crap out of us!

Our group chose to have lunch with the same people all the way through junior high and high school, sometimes adding a person or two. Lunch time was usually filled with laughter. We teased each other about everything. In high school, we were rather relentless with Chris because we liked to see her blush so easily. Her mother performed a "slip check" every day before she left the house. Most of us had those darn half-slips that forever seemed to show, no matter how many times we rolled them. Chris's mom would not allow her to wear one. She had to have a full slip every single day. She also had funny stories about buying bras with her mom. Everything was just funny back then. And so innocent!

The more I hung out with my junior high girlfriends, the less I needed the Dawning Gang. I think I stopped seeing that gang when I was around fifteen. Soon, all of us went to James Ford Rhodes High School, but then, I was no longer in class with my friends. I was on the "academically talented" track, and they all went into the "business" track. Our school was clearly divided into Collegiates or Greasers in those days. Our group fell somewhere in-between. We seemed to get along with almost everyone. I couldn't choose to like people according to how they dressed. I guess I have to admit, I did have a bias against the "rich kids" from our class who modeled for the department stores. Our group still had lunch and attended all the sporting events together. We traveled on the spirit busses to the away games and had a blast. We led cheers, made signs, and did our share of screaming. Back then Rhodes had a #1 basketball team, so it was really exciting. Also, I convinced my friends to play on intraschool sport teams with me so all of us could earn our chenille letter "R." Other teams usually beat us, but not one team had more fun than ours. And by graduation time, everyone in our group had that letter.

At that awkward age in junior high, and even into high school, our all-female group's pajama parties were our best social event. We just couldn't wait for the next one. There we ate, played rock-n-roll, sang, and danced with each other. Dressed up in blankets and sheets, as our formal gowns, we taught each other to slow dance. Silly prank phone calls were made. We talked about boys and shared our life dreams. Then someone pretended to read palms or tell fortunes, and we held seances with a Ouija Board. We snuck out and went for walks in our sleepwear and that was not a time when people wore pajamas everywhere like they do now. We just thoroughly enjoyed ourselves. Mostly we laughed and laughed. Funny, I don't recall us ever sharing much about our home lives. I know I didn't. I was thrilled our senior year when I finally had the opportunity to host our last overnight party because I lived in a home that welcomed my friends.

Teddi was the only one of my friends with access to a car in high school. I didn't drive until I was married at age 23. Teddi received her driver's license as soon as she turned sixteen and drove her mother's Rambler. Mern, Teddi, and I would go downtown and pick up sailors who were just getting off the ship on leave. We were a little bit wild. One time, Sam, a sailor from Dayton, sent me a friendship ring in the mail. We had picked him up a few months earlier and then corresponded through letters. He asked if I would be engaged to him. I was only fifteen or sixteen years old. I wasn't getting engaged to anybody; especially someone I didn't even know. I was afraid he was getting too serious, so I never sent him another letter. Mern's sailor was Kenneth, but he didn't write back to her. I can't believe I remember those names after all these years. I still have that little friendship band in my jewelry box.

If we weren't with Teddi we walked just about everywhere. Sometimes we went all the way downtown on a bus. I don't recall ever being in my father's car except when he made a trip to a tiny grocery store that was about 20 minutes away. The owners were friends of his and gave him credit until payday. He never drove us to a doctor or dentist in all the years I lived with my father. Luckily, I was fairly healthy. And when I was sick, I just wasn't! We weren't allowed to be sick. And we were all very fortunate to have good teeth. I never saw a dentist until I was 18 and my wisdom teeth acted up. By then I had already left home.

At age sixteen, I finally decided to ask my father for permission to date when this kid in my trig class asked me out. I had been seeing boys, but this guy had a car and I wanted him to pick me up at home. Bruce was just one-half year ahead of me, in the January class. He and my father, got along too well to my liking. They both did some television and radio repair work, so they had a lot to talk about. Bruce also took me to meet his parents before we saw Dustin Hoffman in *The Graduate* that night. The poor guy was embarrassed by some of the scenes in the movie and apologized repeatedly. I really liked him a lot. We went out several months, exchanged notes at school, sat next to each other in class, and hung out as much as we could together. Folk Club was an activity we both enjoyed. Bruce had a great voice and played guitar. He was on television singing "The Cruel War" during the Vietnam Conflict. Unfortunately, due to a misunderstanding, we broke up before summer. Once again, I was crushed by a boy! A few weeks after that I met Jim Wyman. Bruce and I, however, remained friends for a long time. Jim and I even doubled with my friend Kathy and Bruce for our prom. Bruce eventually ended up marrying Kathy.

CHAPTER 12

Moving On

Faith is taking the first step,
even when you don't see the whole staircase.
~Martin Luther King, Jr.~

At age seventeen I had it with my father! Fran was already gone. She received a full scholarship to Case Western Reserve two years earlier and never came back home to live. I do remember her coming home just once for a short visit, like winter break, because I recall she played some beautiful French music in our bedroom. I believe the song was called Je t'Aime and I thought it was the most alluring song I had ever heard. At any rate, I reached a breaking point with my father, and took all that I was willing to take. That same summer it was my turn to work at Dawning playground. Little did I know I would meet my future husband, Jim Wyman, there. Jim was the coach on the playground, and I was hired as an assistant. My job was to help put up the long-chained swings on a high ladder, organize craft materials, and help with the sports teams.

Wyman swept me off my feet. He was full of life and fun. Jim used to see me walking to work. With his car windows down, he blasted Momma Cass's music as he pulled right up on the sidewalk in front of me. He was five years older than me, graduated from college, and had already completed his first year of law school. I was just going to be a senior in high school. I never thought he would be interested in a kid like me. Jim was different than anyone I had ever met. We laughed a lot. At dinner time we had a one-hour break, and he took me to his house to go swimming nearly daily. His family had a beautiful in-ground pool in their huge yard. Jim's mom always had dinner waiting for us after our swim. We'd quickly eat and rush back to work. Nothing was going on except exactly that.

My father often sent June, Mern's sister, up to the playground to spy on me. She exaggerated the relationship and I got in a lot of trouble. So, kind of like Bonnie Raitt's song, "Something to Talk About" I found myself beginning to really like Jim. After a short time, my father accused me of all kinds of things and called me a whore. This time I knew what the word meant! And we really weren't even kissing! I asked how he could call me such a name after all the things he had done to me. I packed up and left home that weekend, never to return. I clearly remember my brother, Frank Jr., who was fifteen, cried and asked, "So you're just going to leave me here?" I cried, too, but I left anyway.

Suddenly, there I was—hauling two garbage bags containing all the belongings I could carry, and no place to live. I hadn't seen my mother in a good while. She didn't even have a phone. I happened to have her address because two years prior, she had sent a note telling me that my half-sister, Gail, graduated from nursing school. So, I just showed up at her doorstep. I hadn't lived with my mother since I was four and I really didn't know her, or anything about her, but it was a place to live. Unfortunately, she stayed downtown, in one-bedroom with a shared bathroom down the hall. I called the smelly place "Wino Hotel." It was located on East 22nd and Euclid Ave. Her building was eventually torn down to make way for Cleveland State University. The place was full of unusual characters, to say the least. My mother, May, worked at a Chinese restaurant and brought me food from there. Sometimes she used a hotplate to make a can of soup or hot tea. It definitely wasn't a healthy way to eat, or to live.

Once when Mern came to visit me at May's, we were watching TV, when suddenly a guy peered in through the back window. We lived on the third floor! He had climbed up the fire escape onto the balcony. Mern and I screamed. Not May, she grabbed a broom and went out there to beat the guy and chased him down off that balcony. He never came back and we laughed the rest of the night.

Another time, Mern and I went to see a movie with my mother. Some weirdo came into the dark theater and sat right next to my mother. Suddenly, he put his hand on her thigh. May just very calmly yelled out, "If you don't take your hand off my leg you will be very sorry." The man got up and ran out of the theater. May was quite brave in her own way.

I lived with my mother for just about two months. Meanwhile, my playground friend, Carol, had been in Germany for the summer. When she came home, she and Holly convinced their mother to let me live with them. Amazingly, their house at 5213 Biddulph Avenue, was right across the street from my high school. I would no longer need to take two busses to get to school each morning. Living in a cozy home with the three of them and their Uncle Mickey was a luxury I wasn't used to. I even had my own bedroom for the first time in my life. Mrs. Krailo, Carol and Holly's mother, worked at my high school on the night shift cleaning staff. Before she went to work, she had dinner prepared with directions for completing it. Every evening we sat down together and shared a meal with pleasant conversations. Mrs. Krailo also made a hot breakfast for us every morning. I learned how to eat a soft-boiled egg in a tiny little glass before going to school. I wasn't accustomed to this kind of life and felt very fortunate. So this was how a normal family lived together?

To this day, I am extremely grateful to their family for taking such good care of me and I genuinely love them. However, somehow, I have never felt like an equal to Carol and Holly. I was five years younger, but they always seemed much more sophisticated and better educated than I was. I forever saw myself as inferior to them. I don't think it was anything they did, but rather, it was more about the way I felt about myself. Carol and Holly were major positive influences on my life; they mentored me over many years, but we just never seemed to be on the same level. While living with them, I did begin to realize that my life was changing for the better and my future was going to be very happy. I definitely credit them for this change in my attitude.

I was dating Jim by then. Carol and Holly were not at all thrilled because he was so much older, but they really knew they couldn't stop me. They thought our relationship would limit my personal growth. Living with them, I had rules, a curfew, and responsibilities. I felt loved and very safe. When I first went to live with Carol and Holly, they thought it would only be fair if I would stay with my mother a few times on the weekends. I definitely didn't want to, but I felt obligated, since she had allowed me to move in with her in an emergency. Those visitations didn't last too long.

One time while staying at May's, I was sound asleep when suddenly, there was a knock at the door. It was my mother's creepy boyfriend, Tex. I was very familiar with him because he was constantly hanging out with my mother. I answered the door, and he came right into the room. Before I knew what was happening, that disgusting man was forcing himself upon me. I told him I'd scream if he didn't get up. He put his filthy hand over my mouth. That's when I kicked him where no man wants to be kicked. It worked! He was seething and left in a hurry. Hopefully, he was in a lot of pain. I packed up my little overnight bag and left there as fast as I could. I never told May because I thought absolutely no good could come of it. However, that was my last visit to my mother's place.

When I came home a day early, Carol and Holly were shocked to see me. I explained what happened and said I was never going back there. The tears rolled and I was shaking all over. Finally, I also told them about my father's abuse. For the first time in my entire life I shared the story of my molestation! I had kept that dirty secret locked inside of me for so many years. I had told no one! When Jim came over that day, they had me tell him also. I must admit, I had a deep sense of relief when I let that terrible story out. I had been silent for too many years. Now I felt free. Later, when my children were born, I made sure they never met Frank Bohner Sr.

My senior year in high school was awesome. I was the editor of the front page of our school newspaper. That was a big responsibility and I loved it. We had a blast yet worked very hard to publish *The Rhodes Review*. On numerous occasions we had to leave school because it was lock-up time for the evening. The entire newspaper staff would just walk across the street to my new home, where we would finish up to meet our deadline. Finally, I wasn't embarrassed and could bring friends into my home. That was a big deal to me!

I had genuine school spirit and loved attending football and basketball games to support our teams. I was active in intramural sports, but back then females could not compete against other schools in anything. We only played other classmates. Oh my gosh, I just remembered we weren't even allowed to wear pants to school. During the 1960s in the Cleveland Public Schools, girls had to wear skirts that came to their knees. If your skirt didn't touch the floor upon kneeling, you were sent home to change. Mind you, that was when the miniskirts were very popular. I was sent home more than once, but I usually just had to go across the street.

The first time I was sent home for a short skirt, I was still staying downtown with May. I explained to the teacher that I couldn't go home and was sent to the principal's office. J.J. Stillinger was a very compassionate guy. I told him where I lived and why I would never make it home and back in time. Living outside your school district was not acceptable then. You had to pay tuition or transfer. Also, I was not living with a legal guardian. After a long talk and more than a few tears, Mr. Stillinger took me under his wing and promised to watch out for me. He allowed me to stay at Rhodes for my senior year of high school. When I graduated in 1969, Mr. Stillinger even awarded me a special service commendation at the end of the school year. I was a chairperson who ran a student-only cafeteria lunch period at our high school. In addition to that, Mr. Stillinger wrote a personal letter to a friend of his at The Ohio State University, regarding how I was deserving of financial aid for college. He was a good man who genuinely cared. I was fortunate to have him in my corner.

Chapter 13

Working at Hiram House Camp

Do not go where the path may end.
Go instead where there is no path and lead.
~Ralph Waldo Emerson~

n the spring of my last year in high school, Carol and Holly found a camp counselor program that we thought would be interesting. I went through the training after never having one camping experience in my entire life. Learning was so much fun that I loved the program and everything about it. Each activity was exciting and enjoyable. I learned how to make a bedroll, start a one-match fire, row a boat, fish, tie knots, and shoot a bow and arrow. We saddled our own horses and learned to ride. We cooked and sang songs around a campfire, and then slept out under the stars. Our arts and craft projects were created from nature. I soaked it all in like a little kid. Soon I had the credentials to be a camp counselor. I was hired on the spot and given a summer job at a resident camp called Hiram House.

What a perfect opportunity. I had a chance to make new friends, pass on my knowledge, learn responsibility, and have the greatest time of my life outdoors. Hiram House Camp was an amazing place! The summer schedule consisted of one and two-week residential sessions, and then a special week at the end of each summer. I worked with the Pioneer Girls, who were ages 7–12 for two years as a group counselor. I did everything along with my campers so I could learn more and hone my camping skills. I wanted to be a great counselor and lead by example. We had daily inspections of our log cabin living quarters, performed by the camp nurse. For inspection, everyone had to have neat, clean cabins and stars were given out to the best cabin each day. Making your bed with hospital corners was a must!

I was quite happy to have a nurse right there at the camp. For someone who was rarely ever sick in grade school and high school, suddenly, I found myself ill quite often. It seemed like I was always sick with a sore throat, or bronchitis from sleeping out in the dampness and the campers coughing on me. Poison ivy was another problem. Somehow, I was a poison ivy magnet. I seemed to get it every other week. Guess that just shows I wasn't afraid to hike on paths less taken. I loved the woods.

We all got up very early to the sound of a loud clanging bell. Color guards for the flag ceremony were chosen from the inspection winners and the flag was posted at a morning ceremony each day. All campers and counselors ate three meals daily in the huge mess hall, unless they were on an overnight sleep-out. When groups finished eating, they would start a camp song and soon everyone would join in. It was a great way to wake up. Everyone was so happy, at least until night-time when a lot of little ones cried from homesickness.

Camp counselors worked extremely hard with almost no down-time. You were essentially responsible for the lives, education, entertainment, and well-being of your group. There were several activities that were somewhat stressful, where accidents could easily happen. The pool, horse stables, boating on the lake, hiking in the creek, fishing, and overnights with campfires and small wild animals were a few of those activities where safety was a serious issue.

Late at night, after all campers were asleep, us counselors could go out for a short break, if we weren't on Night Duty and had to remain with the kids. We sometimes went into Chagrin Falls for a burger or pizza. But usually, we were so exhausted we went to bed shortly after the campers. We had to keep notes on the kids because at the end of each session we were not allowed to go anywhere until we wrote a full report on each camper. No computers then; just old-fashioned typewriters and a great deal of whiteout.

I absolutely loved Final Night for each camp session. All the groups gathered around a huge bonfire. They had to lead a song, perform a skit, read stories, or perform in any other way they saw fit. So much creativity, laughter, and wholesome fun. Each summer, the staff also put on a big production that was written by one of the counselors. My favorite was a parody of *Jesus Christ, Superstar*. "Majaska, Superstar" was a huge hit. Majaska was the legendary character who roamed the woods of Hiram House Camp for decades. He was usually the subject of all the scary campfire stories. I guess he was kind of the Boogeyman of the camp. The counselor did a fabulous job writing parodies for the most popular songs. I had the lead female role, Wagampo, an Indian squaw who was in love with Majaska. I had to sing "I Don't Know How to Love Him" as well as other songs. My fellow counselors had a surprise in store for me. Just as I finished my solo, they tied me to the pole, and a little too enthusiastically for my liking, painted me with honey! I felt that dripping, sticky goo from head to toe as I was fed to the wolves! No one told me that was going to happen. Of course, the audience loved it! I had no choice but to be a good sport about it. That's something you just don't forget; especially trying to wash that gross honey out of long hair.

I went off the high dive my first week at camp. At the beginning, I wasn't afraid in the least. I repeatedly jumped off and loved it. Only the next day, when my thighs were completely black-and-blue, did I develop a fear of the height of that board. I should have gone right back up, but I gave my legs about a week to heal. The next time I went up I froze. I developed a serious fear of getting hurt. I couldn't jump off that high dive, no matter how hard I tried. I ended up going down the long ladder. After encouragement and pep talks from so many kind people I tried again. I was determined, but it didn't work. I had five summers to attempt it, but I just couldn't do it. My new fear was greater than my desire and I never went off that high dive again.

When I was eighteen, I stayed at Hiram House Camp an extra week because I needed more money to buy my first contact lenses. The very last week of each summer was saved for "Dedrater Camp." That was "retarded" backwards. At that time, the phrase "mentally retarded" was still used to describe people who are now called "intellectually disabled." I recall the instant the bus pulled up and the campers filed off looking right at us. I had led a somewhat sheltered life and was ignorant of a lot of things. These campers ranged in ages 7–50 years of age. They had helmets, crutches, braces, thick glasses, hearing aids, and wheelchairs. They also had strange ways of walking and talking. I turned to Charlie, my boss, and said, "I don't think I can do this." He laughed, hugged me, and replied, "If you don't fall in love with these campers by the end of the week, I will double your last paycheck." Charlie knew exactly what he was talking about.

My job was to hold music class with small groups of campers. It was without a doubt, the most fun I had all summer! Those campers loved singing, marching, banging on instruments, and just having a good time. It was easy to make them happy. I learned so much about Down syndrome, epilepsy, sight and hearing impairments, and other special needs in children and adults. The week ended too quickly. As the campers filed onto the bus, I was crying. They had sincerely touched my heart. Charlie was absolutely right. He didn't have to double my paycheck.

Working at Hiram House Camp impacted my life greatly. I was a counselor for two years and then became the Unit Leader in charge of all counselors and campers in our age group for the next three summers. It was such a positive experience that I thought about going back on a volunteer basis when I was older. Instead, I worked with children in a different way.

CHAPTER 14

The Ohio State Days

I think, therefore I am.
~René Descartes~

My very first airplane ride was a short one from Cleveland to Columbus, Ohio. Carol and Holly gifted me with airline tickets to go to my freshman orientation at The Ohio State University. I could hardly believe I was going to college! During my senior year of high school, I boldly marched into a guidance counselor's office. I told her that nobody had called me down for an appointment, but I wanted to go to college. She didn't even attempt to hold back her surprise at my statement. She knew nothing about me. I understood that we had 400 students in our graduating class, so her workload was overwhelming. Seems she only dealt with the top students who were in all the honors classes and the activities that received attention. I was not in any honors classes and considered myself to be an average student.

That guidance counselor simply asked where I wanted to go. I had hardly even heard of many colleges, so I named three that I was aware of: Ohio State, Ohio University, and Ohio Wesleyan, where Carol and Holly had gone. She said, "Pick one and we'll begin." I picked Ohio State off the top of my head. That started the process. Had I not walked into her office, I perhaps would not have ended up in college. Our school counselors didn't do much to encourage average kids like me.

I was happy with my choice and I had a blast at OSU. That's probably why I got my share of D's in three classes. Teddi went with me, and we had four people to a room and four rooms to a suite. Out of our suitemates, Teddi, Freddie, Marty, and I (all females) hung out together. I was the only one to make it through the first year and in the end, the only one to graduate. Suddenly, having total freedom to make all your own decisions wasn't so easy for everyone. I still had the goal to become a teacher, so that carrot was always dangling in front of me. I never lost sight of it, no matter how hard it was. That freshman year we did some studying and so much reading! I didn't really know how to study. I read everything, retained very little, and highlighted entirely too many words. I thought everything was new information and important. Needless to say, I was not at all prepared to pass exams. Some of those freshman requirement classes were held in an auditorium with 500 or more students. I usually sat up in the balcony where I learned very little. It was easy to get lost in the crowd. Although, I did love my philosophy class in that auditorium. I was pleasantly surprised to see that it held my full attention, even from the balcony.

I was on the Dean's List for academic probation one quarter, but that woke me up. I had worked too hard to get there. After all, I had some grants, a scholarship, a loan, and a Work-Study job. I couldn't lose all that. I forged May's signature on my financial aid application because I couldn't get either parent to fill out the documents. My father was on disability and my mother was a part-time waitress, so it wasn't difficult to qualify. I just had to complete the forms myself and sign her name to those papers. I was determined so that's exactly what I did. By the next year, I had filed emancipation papers from both parents, so I was on my own and no longer needed their signatures.

College was a tough adjustment for many young adults. OSU was definitely a school where students believed in partying. Just the simple fact that the main street from one end of the campus to the other was called "High Street" made us feel obligated to drink. I started college in 1969. During those days, eighteen-year-olds could drink 3.2 beer. It was like a lite beer, a little watered down. Sure, we didn't care. We just drank more of it, going from one bar to the next to experience as many places as possible in one night. High Street was full of bars, so we never made it to all of them. We sang a lot of "Hang on Sloopy", "Nah Nah Nah Nah- Hey, Hey, Goodbye", and "Does Anybody Really Know What Time it is?" The last bar always sent us running because we did have a curfew and would get locked out of the dorm. When that happened, you had to call the Floor Resident Advisor. My RA's name was Robin and I recall that she didn't like me. She thought I was a real troublemaker on the floor, and she had the power to get us evicted from the dorm. I was tired of being accused of things I didn't do, so I tried to stay clear of her radar.

I had two work assignments at college. My first one was a receptionist or clerk in a Postgraduate Studies office. There were seven professors and dozens of students working on their Ph.D.'s. The hardest part about that job was reciting all seven of the professor's names every time I answered the phone. Remember, at that time you spoke to real people. There was no "If you want to speak with Dr. X, dial 1. If you want to speak with Dr. Z, dial 2." The place was usually crazy, yet lots of fun. Someone was constantly defending an oral dissertation, taking written exams, meeting with their advisors, or just crying due to the immense pressure and stress. I wasn't sure how to handle it. I had never seen so many adults cry!

My second job was at the OSU Student Center in the bowling alley. Other than having to spray those sweaty, smelly bowling shoes, I loved that job. I checked people in, collected payments, and organized shoes. I was able to bowl for free before or after work. I usually bowled about three games and seemed to get worse with each one. But it was fun.

The twin towers, Lincoln and Morrill, were right next to the OSU Football Stadium. Those dorms were only a few years old, but already had the reputation to be called Sodom and Gomorrah; two "sinful" cities mentioned in the *Bible*. They were the first coed dorms on campus. With 23 floors and housing nearly 2,000 students each, they seemed more like giant hotels to me. I confess, it was a lot of fun living there.

Even though we were right next to the stadium in Morrill Tower, I disliked football. I didn't have any interest in buying student tickets for the games. My perspective was that everything was about football, and I was resentful of that fact. I did go to one game during my four years in college. It was absolutely crazy. The stadium holds 100,000 people and it was full. OSU was number one back then with Woody Hayes as their coach. There was so much excitement and hype around the games, and I didn't want any part of it. I guess I missed out on a lot. Or maybe I didn't. I had a great deal of fun; it just didn't revolve around sports, although Teddi and I did buy season tickets to the basketball games.

I had some great visitors my first year at school. Though Jim and I were madly in love, I didn't let him come down to see me for two months. I thought I had to first acclimate to college life on my own. That was a very long two months! Late fall, some of my junior high girlfriends came to see me. They flew down to Columbus, like I had done for orientation. We had such a fun weekend; like one of our old pajama parties! None of them went to college, so I think they really enjoyed the experience of seeing what college life was like. It's funny, but I was a little envious of them, because they were all working and making money already. My girlfriends could travel, go out together, and do whatever they wanted. I was in school.

Freshman year, Teddi and I drove to New York City for spring break. Her sister lived in Queens, so we had a good time in NYC doing all the touristy things. We were involved in an accident while riding in a yellow taxicab. We were on the way home from a bar where we had Long Island ice-teas for the first time. That was something we noticed immediately upon arriving in New York City. Every single cab had numerous dents! They drove aggressively and seemed to push their way in and out of tiny spaces. We saw *Hello Dolly,* on Broadway, starring Phyllis Diller. Teddi and I went to the top of the Empire State Building. The weather did not permit us to ride on the Staten Island Ferry to view the Statue of Liberty. We went downtown to see all the skyscrapers and we even shopped in a few big department stores. New York was way too crowded for me. People were not as friendly as they were at home. It seemed like everyone was rushing about and bumping into us. Unlike most people, I did not love New York.

Shortly after returning from spring break, we began to notice a lot of protests taking place all around the country. We were pretty naive and kept on going about our business. There is some honest truth in the notion that academia sits among ivory towers. Then suddenly, one day it came right onto our campus. Students, as well as outsiders, were protesting the Vietnam War. They thought the US had no business in that country. I remember coming out of class and a school reporter asked my opinion about the ongoing OSU protest. I didn't even know there was one! I really had no clue but gave some sort of diplomatic answer about compromise on the part of the administration. It was printed in *The Lantern*, our school paper, and I felt stupid. I needed to learn about what was going on. Things got worse in the next few days and the Columbus Police were called in to handle the protestors. They all wore intimidating riot gear with bullet proof vests and helmets with gas masks. They covered their torsos with large, clear shields while wielding billy clubs. My friends and I decided to go up to the demonstration area and see for ourselves what was happening. It was easy to become "one of them" without intending to do so. Before I knew what was happening, an officer tossed a tear gas cannister our way. Part of it cut my leg as it exploded. That just made us mad, so now I was also protesting!

The next day, the university cancelled classes. I took advantage of it and went home to see Jim. While I was there, I received a phone call from Teddi that OSU was formally closed down and everyone had to go home immediately. I later found out that was due to the Kent State shootings by the National Guard. I just cried and cried. I couldn't explain it, but I felt guilty and partially responsible for those students being killed because I had participated in the protests at my school. I felt like we had encouraged others to do the same. Truthfully, I know it wasn't my fault, but I was horrified those students could be shot just for their beliefs. By the time our university reopened, we were under the watch of the National Guard. It was extremely intimidating. Fortunately, that was short-lived, because summer break was in a few weeks. What an interesting, eye-opening first year of college!

Freshmen and sophomores were required to live in a dorm. I lived in Morrill Tower those first two years, and the third year, I moved into an apartment. Our friend Marty was pregnant, so she got married and moved back home. My old roommates, Teddi and Freddie had returned to Columbus but were not back in school; they were working. The three of us got an off-campus apartment. That didn't work out too well, seeing as I was the only student.

It was my junior year, so I really had to buckle down if I wanted to graduate within the four years. I had already been accepted into the College of Education. The process was competitive at that time. We had to fill out an extensive application, write a long essay, take a written exam, and go through a committee interview just to get into education. That was all done before my junior year. Now I had to get serious, and I needed some peace and quiet. I ended up going back on campus to the library daily to achieve that.

We did have some fun at that apartment though. Teddi taught us how to make homemade pierogies. That was a lot of hard work. Our backs suffered from all the bending over the table, but they were inexpensive to make and very delicious. She helped us make potato with cheese and sauerkraut pierogies. After pan frying the tasty, filled dumplings in butter, she topped them with sautéed onions and sour cream. That girl loved to cook!

But one thing Teddi absolutely could not cook was hard boiled eggs! Nearly every single morning before work, Teddi boiled eggs for her egg salad sandwiches. Inevitably, she fell back asleep, and I often woke up to eggs exploding in the kitchen. That burnt sulfur smell filled the entire apartment constantly. It happened all the time. Teddi never learned to stay awake when her eggs were cooking. At least no apartment fire ever occurred, so I guess it was just funny.

Finally, my senior year, I rented an apartment by myself. It was nice to live alone, just off campus. My bike helped me to get anywhere I needed to go. I had to carry it up and down a steep flight of stairs because I lived on the second floor, but it was worth it. By then, I was finishing up my coursework to become a teacher. Elementary teachers need to train in a wide variety of experiences. The first quarter of my senior year, I had to take piano and recorder. Ugh! The recorder I could handle, but that piano was worse than my violin experience. Without a place to practice anywhere, I received a D on my final exam, and I still recall the professor saying that was because I never missed a class. Glad he didn't fail me. Luckily, I had done extremely well on the recorder and all my weekly quizzes in that class.

I also had an art class where we had to make sculptures and paintings. I pretty much sucked at both, but I got through it. I had already completed my art appreciation class and aced it. That way of dealing with art I could handle. I student taught a fifth-grade class in Columbus, during the second quarter of my senior year. I loved the entire experience! Somehow, I made the Dean's List before I graduated. And this time it was the good list.

One day a surprise visitor showed up at my apartment; it was, my mother, May! That was a shocker! I think she had been visiting my half-brother, Bruce, in Columbus. I don't know how or why she came, but we spent a couple days together. That's when she taught me how to make chili. I believe that is the only thing my mother ever taught me in my entire life. Well, maybe I do credit her for my survival instincts.

During my senior year in college, I found a guy who drove to Cleveland every weekend. He was married and his wife stayed in Cleveland. Every Friday he drove a carload of us and made a little cash. I stayed at Jim's apartment on Coventry with him and his roommate, Michael Grodach, until Sunday, when our guy made the return trip back to school. It was perfect. Much cheaper and nicer than the Greyhound busses I had tried a few times.

Every Sunday it was difficult to go back, but I was getting closer and closer to my goal. I did what I had to do and finished in four years because I had big plans. I do have a cool yearbook which shows all the hippie styles back then. Somehow, due to my own quirky personal protests, I chose not to put my picture in it! Just the same way I decided not to attend my college graduation. It was different then. There were over a thousand education majors. They would simply say "Would all the Education Majors please rise?" Blah, blah, blah… "Move your tassels to the other side." I decided not to participate and go straight home for my last summer at Hiram House Camp.

CHAPTER 15

My Brief Marriage

People change and forget to tell each other.
~William Hellman~

Just two months after graduating from OSU, I was married to Jim Wyman. We picked out rings together and were engaged 6 months prior, on Valentine's Day. I worked at the camp until a few days before the wedding. On August 4, 1973, we had a ceremony in Jim's parents' Brooklyn Heights backyard. Currently, that property is where my daughter, Lyndie, her husband, Rocky, and three of my grandkids live. It's a beautiful, huge yard with a wooded area. Neither of us were religious people so we agreed to create our own ceremony and hold it outdoors. Jim and I exchanged our vows privately in the woods on the property, at Shallow Rock. Reverend Richter, from Brooklyn Heights United Church of Christ, and Sister Juanita Shealey oversaw the wedding. Reverend Richter gave the benediction at the end. Sister Juanita performed a reading from Kahlil Gibran's book, *The Prophet*.

The Vietnam War was in full force. Young men were being drafted for mandatory military service. Jim's draft number was something like thirty-four, so he definitely would have been called up to fight in that horrible conflict. Only a few draft deferments kept people from going. One of them was "holding an essential civilian job." At that time, teaching was considered one of those jobs. Jim went to teach elementary school for a few years at St. Aloysius Catholic School. Sister Juanita was his boss, the school principal. That job kept him from going to war. Sister Juanita became a very close family friend and eventually, became our daughter Lyndie's Godmother at her christening.

Our wedding was extremely casual. Even my "wedding gown" came right off a rack at the department store for something like $39! It was a beautiful cream-colored, long cotton voile dress with tiny little purple flowers on it. The gown was an empire waist, which was very popular at the time. I had long hair hanging down and sandals. Typical hippie look. Just cake and champagne were served to about 150 guests. All my closest junior high and high school friends were there, as were most of the camp staff. Also in attendance were all of Jim's friends and family members. Of course, Mern was a bridesmaid. She was seven months pregnant with Jennifer, her second child. Holly was there, but Carol was in Germany for the summer. Surprisingly, my fifth-grade teacher, Mrs. Oschek was able to make it. Fran was already living in Bermuda, but Frank Jr. was in attendance. My father was not invited. This is terrible, but I must confess, I don't even remember if my mother was there or not. WOW! How sad is that?

The year was 1973 and I was 23 years old. Seems young now to get married, but it wasn't then. Jim had actually asked me to marry him the first year we dated. I was still in high school. I told him I had to go to college, and he'd have to take a raincheck. He understood and waited.

Our honeymoon was quite an adventure. We drove 6,000 miles in two weeks, heading west and then north into Canada. We saw Yellowstone and the Badlands, rode on car ferries, and pitched a tent everywhere we went. We camped on grass, sand, marble cliffs, and even red dirt on Prince Edward Island. We went as far as Lake Louise and Banff. The scenery was absolutely fabulous, but we were forever exhausted. Toward the last part of our trip, I ended up in the ER in Canada, with acute tonsillitis.

Jim drove straight home through Michigan, while I slept in the backseat. I picked up my head only long enough to see Sault St. Marie for about two seconds.

I didn't get a teaching job right away. I had been interviewed at Ohio State and promised a letter of commitment from Cleveland Public Schools. Unfortunately, my recruiter died during the summer and his list of prospective teachers was lost. So, the entire summer went by without a word about a teaching job.

First, I worked at a downtown employment agency; a job I found in a newspaper ad. That was not a good fit. I was much more of a social worker than a salesperson. I tended to tell people how to get a job on their own without paying the agency fee. That didn't work! The company was incredibly happy when I quit after just one month. No doubt, they would have fired me. Next, I worked at the May Company, a department store in downtown Cleveland. I sold cosmetics and perfumes. I loved that job and they offered to make me a buyer for the company. But I knew I wanted to teach, so I briefly became a teacher's aide in a Cleveland school, hoping to get my foot in the door.

Meanwhile, Jim also worked downtown when we were first married. By then he had graduated from Case Western Reserve's Law School. He was the Law Clerk for Federal Judge Leroy Conte. Life was good! We bought a house when we got married in the Old Brooklyn area of Hillcrest and South Hills. Finally, I learned to drive, and we bought another car. I'll admit, I dented more than one door or bumper. I had a lot of trouble judging the passenger side on those big cars. Over time, I became a good driver.

However, when we took road trip vacations, Wyman insisted on doing all the driving. He liked being in control. Flying, where he would have no control, was out of the question. We enjoyed the Canadian wilderness and the Georgian Bay—always camping. Once, we drove all the way to the Florida Keys and rendezvoused with Mern and her husband, Steve. Mern and I were both mommies and travelled with our seven-month-olds. I remember it rained a lot and when it didn't, we got very sunburned. The baby girls were fine. They were kept in the shade and wore cute little sun bonnets. I recall how much we enjoyed the crab, lobster, fried clams, and other fresh seafood in the Florida Keys.

Marriage was good for a while; until it wasn't. We did a lot of things together and separately. We enjoyed the theater, movies, concerts, and sports events. I bowled and golfed in leagues and Jim played on multiple softball teams. We had lots of friends and somehow our house became the neighborhood hangout. Matt, Dean, and Robby, teens who lived right nearby, hung out at our house nearly every evening. We played poker, pinochle, and rummy card games. We were constantly competing in the old board games like Scrabble, Clue, Monopoly, and Risk. We never got tired of games or of challenging one another.

Jim and I also had three different people live with us during our first year of marriage. We both enjoyed helping others when we were able. His friend, Carl, was going through a divorce. Next, was Jim's lawyer friend who lived in Findlay, Ohio but worked in downtown Cleveland. He went home on the weekends to his wife. Lastly, was my brother, Frank. He was brilliant and received a full four-year ride to Marietta College. Unfortunately, he flunked out at the end of his freshman year. Sadly, my brother was diagnosed with paranoid schizophrenia when his behavior became bizarre and unsafe. He had to be institutionalized.

We moved into our new house in March of 1979. One month later, when the kids were asleep, we went out onto our new balcony to look at the full moon. Suddenly, Jim turned to me and told me there was no love in our relationship. It was as if someone hit me with a sledgehammer. My response was something like, "What the fuck are you talking about?"

I soon came to learn that his statement actually translated into, "I met someone else, and I want out of this marriage." On December 20, 1979, our divorce was finalized. We were married only seven years. G.J. had just turned two and Lyndie was a bit over three years old. Two months later, in February, Jim and Cindy were married.

CHAPTER 16

My Kids

The best way to predict the future is to create it.
~Abe Lincoln~

ern and I were pregnant together the entire nine months. This was my first baby and Mern's third. During my fourth year of marriage Melynda Leah Wyman was born. Mern and I had the same ob-gyn, Dr. Pop-Lazic, from Deaconess hospital. It was fun going to appointments and then out to dinner each time we saw the doctor. At some point during the pregnancy, Jim and I had seen *Finian's Rainbow* and one of the characters was named Melinda. That was it! If we had a girl, she was to be named Melinda, and Leah, after Jim's mom. At that time, there were no ultra sound tests that notified us of the baby's gender. So we just had to wait and see. I made the mistake of telling Mern that name choice. Her beautiful baby girl was born just two weeks before mine. Mern stole the name. I was infuriated! I guess she honestly thought it would be cool if our daughters had the same name. I didn't think it was cool at all. So, when my daughter was born on her due date, August 23, 1976, we named her Melynda, with the different spelling, and called her Lyndie. She was gorgeous, weighed in at 8 pounds, 6 ounces and was very healthy.

I absolutely adored Lyndie, but I found being a new parent was difficult. I was on a two-year maternity leave and missed teaching. Jim decided to quit his job and immediately form a private law practice. In addition, I ended up getting pregnant in Florida when our baby girl was just seven months old. As if that wasn't enough to deal with, Jim also decided to build a house from scratch onto a cliff just down the street from his parents. By the time Lyndie's baby brother was born, Jim was never home. I used to take Lyndie to the house site to see her daddy, while it was being built. We had told her about the woods and creek, down at the bottom of the steep cliff from the property. From then on, she called the house "Water Down There." Lyndie loved seeing the construction site and asked every day if we could go see Water Down There. But that house had become my enemy. I couldn't compete with it, nor with Jim's obsession over it.

I loved being with Lyndie because she was always so happy and just as cute as could be. Lyndie was an intelligent baby and learned quite easily. We sang a lot, read tons of books, and walked with the stroller. When it was warm enough, she liked to go in a tiny swimming pool on the front porch. Johnny, the little toddler next door, came over to play with her. When she was in her walker, she held onto our dog's tail. Alack pulled her everywhere, especially back and forth across the porch and Lyndie screamed with pure joy. We named our dog Alack, and our cat Forsooth, from Old English words that show dismay or regret. After Forsooth died, we bought two Siamese cats and named them Bilbo and Frodo. Jim had agreed to have pets, in spite of the fact that he didn't really want any. He understood how important they were to me and that I had to have my animals.

Lyndie was nursed, with no solid foods for five months. Then I strained fresh foods like bananas, carrots, beans, and peas, while supplementing with nursing. You know, the first baby had to eat only the healthiest foods, so I made my own for a short while. Then I got over it. She liked to eat and was not at all picky. Lyndie grew quickly and walked at nine months. Then she was into everything and there was no stopping her. But the one thing that did calm that baby girl down was reading. We spent hours with books or catalogues, especially building her vocabulary.

Before I had a moment to catch my breath, our son was born. Gordon James Wyman was born December 12, 1977. Lyndie called him, "GJ Biney" because that's how she said Wyman. Believe me, G.J. is just happy he was a boy, or his name would have been Annonda Noel. Jim was James Gordon, but he said he didn't want a Jr., so we named our son after Jim's dad. I thought the name Gordon was too strong for a baby, so I said I'd only name him that if we could call him G.J., and we did. He became Gordon when he was in college, but our family still calls him G.J., or just G.

He was also a beautiful baby, but he was born ten days after his due date and was 9 pounds 8 ounces. Most of the new baby clothes and newborn diapers didn't even fit G.J. But boy was he cute! So chunky and healthy! He was also a nursed baby. Sometimes, I felt like a feeding machine. It was really overwhelming to attend to both kids, by myself, all day and evening. I was sleep deprived and not at all taking care of myself. Also, I don't rule out the possibility that I may have suffered from postpartum blues after G.J. was born. Still, I did the same activities with him. G.J., too, was very intelligent and learned easily. He had a great disposition, like his big sister, so he was fun to play with. Of course, he emulated Lyndie, so G. also walked in his ninth month. I could hardly keep up with the two of them.

One morning we were still in bed and awakened by loud laughter and giggling coming out of the kids' bedroom. This was a tiny starter house with only two bedrooms. One room they shared, where we put two cribs on opposite walls. On this particular morning we were shocked to walk in and discover that G.J., at less than a year old, had figured out how to take his jammies and diaper off. He had smeared poop everywhere! Hence, the laughter coming from their room was out of pure entertainment of two impish kids.

First thing in the morning, while Jim got ready for work, I had to bathe both kids, bleach the walls and crib, and take the nasty sheets and blankets downstairs. For safety, I put them both in the playpen in the living room. I dashed down to the basement to throw the dirty things in the washing machine. Coming up the steps, again I heard that same kind of mischievous laughter.

Lyndie had reached up and grabbed the baby powder from the bookshelf. She had stripped her little brother naked and covered him in powder from head to toe. He looked like the Pillsbury Dough Boy, and I could hardly see his eyes. Once again, I had to give G.J. a bath, but this time it was a quick one in the kitchen sink. Then I vacuumed up the powder mess. When the buzzer went off for the laundry, I thought I was clever by closing them both in the dining room. I planned to be gone a total of one minute this time. No noise as I came up the basement steps. No noise because both kids and the dog were lapping up Cheerios as fast as they could. The unopened giant box had been in the middle of the dining table. They emptied the entire box all over the floor! Was it bedtime yet? Not even noon! What a day!

After the divorce, I did a lot with the kids as a single mom. We spent a great deal of time with my friends, Carol and Holly and their husbands, Jim and George. We also hung out with Sandy and Chris and their kids. Other times, we pitched a tent and camped alone, often at Punderson State Park. G.J. never forgave Lyndie for stepping out his first one-match fire when she was losing the contest to see who could get the first burning flames going. Mern went camping with us just one time but was terrified of the raccoons. When Lyndie and G. were nine and eight years old, we drove all the way to Orlando, Florida to meet Fran, Derek, and Kirsten at Disney World. My kids were the best travelers ever! Lots of to-do activities, books, travel games, and snacks made it easy to take them in the car. There were no video games, iPads, or car movie screens back then. The kids and I enjoyed going to parks, movies, the live theater, and circuses.

I recall Lyndie and G.J. did not love going out to sit-down dinners, where they had to behave for much too long to their liking. They did however, love going to the library weekly, just as Fran had done with us. For many years we all read together every night in my bed. Each Sunday we all sat in one big chair and read the comics together. The three of us also tried the church thing for a while, by attending services at The Church in the Woods. When the minister made a home visit, in attempt to persuade me to become a "member" I was done with that!

We did a great deal of traveling and went to Bermuda several times together, starting when Lyndie was only five. Both kids loved traveling, especially taking the airplanes. To this day, they still love the ocean as much as Fran and I do. When I took G.J. to Poland, at age fourteen, I couldn't convince Lyndie to go. Many years later, she and I went on a cruise that went up the Muddy Mississippi. Peter, Paul, and Mary at Blossom Music Center was the kids first concert and we had front row seats. They were young and I had played the album, *Peter, Paul, and Mommy,* so often, that they knew all the songs. Their first opera was *Carmen* because my school had partnered with the Playhouse Square cast to put on a joint production in our building. Then we were given tickets for the real thing. *Carmen* was a bit over their heads so they later enjoyed the live production of *Hansel and Gretel* much more.

CHAPTER 17

Postgraduate Studies at CSU

Your life is what you make it. And nothing,
absolutely nothing, is beyond your reach.
~President Barack Obama~

Shortly after my divorce, I realized it would be very difficult to take care of myself, two kids part-time, and all the bills. I needed more schooling to climb the pay scale. I entered Cleveland State's Graduate School in the College of Education in 1982, while teaching full-time. I enrolled in a program called EMERGADOL, specializing in the curriculum and instruction of adolescents. I thoroughly loved that coursework and the professor, Dr. Ron Tyrrell. It was run like a big group therapy session, where we learned about kids by first learning about ourselves. The program was extremely interesting, and my heart and brain were often tired from learning. We studied Freud, Yung, Gestalt, Maslow, Piaget, Glasser, Cooperative Learning, and Developmental Stages, among a plethora of other topics. We met one evening a week and then, on several full weekends. I remember when I told my kids that I would not see them some weekends and their response was: "We hate Cleveland State!" Talk about a guilt trip! That was the most difficult part of getting my degree, losing time with my kids. I knew it was necessary if I wanted to earn more money to make ends meet.

I received my master's degree and volunteered as a cofacilitator in the EMERGADOL Program for the next several years. Remaining in the world of academia inspired me to go further with my schooling. I enjoyed learning and researching. CSU had just opened a new doctoral studies program called Urban Education. The program allowed inner-city teachers and administrators to become scholars in a comprehensive study of theories and applications. Since I was teaching in the city, I thought it was a perfect fit. I made it into the Fourth Cohort, which for the first time consisted of only half the number of students and all ten of us were females. The college was trying to prove itself, and it was a tough program. One student quit after the first midterm. A second dropped out after the first quarter. The third woman left at the end of three quarters. So only seven of us remained in Cohort IV.

The courses and the amount of reading we had to do were intense. The research and statistical analysis courses on a doctoral level were just crazy. It was like a foreign language to me. We had an exam or a paper to write nearly every single week. The only perk doctoral students received at the time was a private little study cubicle in the library. We met for classes two nights a week and that was after teaching school all day long. Luckily, child care was not a major issue for me because I started the doctoral program in 1990. My kids were already thirteen and fourteen years old. Most of my classes were held on days they spent with their father. When the kids became older, they ended up spending more time at their dad's. He lived in their school district where all their friends and activities were located. I did have to pick and choose which of their sporting events I was able to attend because my schedule was so grueling.

After two years the cohort broke off into our own areas of specialization. I chose the Learning and Development track. It took repeated Comprehensive Exam attempts for me, but I was determined and never entertained the idea of quitting. My written book, the dissertation, was titled "A Multilevel Analysis of the Effects of School and Individual Student

Variables on the Ohio Fourth-Grade Proficiency Test Scores." You know, a Ph.D. rarely says anything concisely. My advisor was Dr. Nancy Klein, an excellent scholar and role-model. Her area of specialization was long-term studies on premature babies at Cleveland's Rainbow Babies and Children's Hospital. She was a very calm person who always helped me to refocus when things got a little crazy. From the beginning, Dr. Klein believed in me and helped to build up my confidence. My methodologist, Dr. Joshua Bagaka's, was brilliant. Joshua was a kind, gentle person from Kenya. Dr. Bagaka's formally chose to spell his surname with an apostrophe because he was proud to be his father's son. He taught me a great deal about research and life. His area of expertise was the hierarchical linear model. Dr. Bagaka's encouraged me to become the very first student at Cleveland State to use such a model for my research analysis. It added an extra year to my studies, but it was worth it to be able to break ground in that area.

This Ph.D. was strictly for me to prove something to myself. I had already maxed out on the teacher's pay scale for educational bonuses in Cleveland schools. I would not receive one extra penny upon completion of this degree. I always knew that my brother and sister were extremely intelligent. Having never considered myself to be a bright student, I wanted to fight for this degree. Facing tough issues in my life was something I was quite used to accomplishing. One thing I definitely knew about myself was that I was not a quitter. So, it took me nearly nine years, but I did become Dr. Patricia K. Wyman on Mother's Day in 1999.

CHAPTER 18

My Teaching Career

Teaching might even be the greatest of all the arts
since the medium is the human mind and spirit.
~John Steinbeck~

It was a long road from the beginning of my teaching career and eventually earning a Ph.D. So, it all goes back to that teacher's aide job I held approximately fifteen years earlier. I kept the job until I realized that my teacher was using me. Because I had a degree in teaching, she made me do all her grunt work. I did her lesson plans and took her kids everywhere so she would not have to leave the classroom. I went outside to recess with her students, and took them to physical education, music, and art classes. I taught all the classes she didn't like. I ran reading groups, graded all their papers, and did anything else she asked me to do. After tolerating being used by that teacher for nearly two months, I decided it was time to get my own classroom.

The school year had already started and still I hadn't heard anything. I went downtown to the Cleveland Board of Education. Fortunately, the secretary was away from her desk on a restroom break because normally, nobody gets past a good secretary. So, I sat down and waited. Suddenly, a woman came out of an office with someone who was leaving. I told her I wanted to teach, but she said I needed to make an appointment. Again, because I am not a quitter, I said I could not leave until she directed me to somebody who would give me a teaching job. I didn't know it at the time, but I was speaking to Norma Tarr. She just happened to be the Supervisor at the top of the Personnel Department. No one was hired without her approval. Ms. Tarr took me into her office and that's when I found out my recruiter's paperwork had been lost. After a lengthy interview she hired me immediately. I walked out of her office grinning ear-to-ear. The following Monday I finally began my teaching career. Although my contracted teaching salary was just around $7,000 that year, I was on cloud nine. I got my foot in the door and my personal fourth-grade goal had become a reality.

At age twenty-four, on October 14, 1974, I proudly walked into my very own classroom at Charles Dickens Elementary School. That first teaching job consisted of a fourth-fifth grade split class. Teaching two grade levels at once was a difficult challenge, for new or experienced teachers. My students were selected by the teachers from four different overcrowded classrooms. You can imagine which students they chose to send. So, I had 40 kids wall-to-wall. I absolutely loved it and that may have been my best teaching year ever. I did have one student permanently removed when he wrote "WHITE BITCH" on the chalkboard. It was just a little too obvious, seeing as I was the only white person in the room. Gutsy move for a new teacher, but I told the principal that child could not be in my classroom because he had no respect for me. The principal knew what the other teachers had dumped on me, so I believe that's the only reason he agreed to meet my request. The student was sent to a more experienced teacher. From then on, I had no problem with my class.

I loved spending every day with that group. Teaching was fun back then. If you taught the required curriculum mandated by the state, you could be as creative as you liked. Over the years, my students and I recorded albums from camp songs, performed skits from our reading books, and held math competitions. We made parachutes and paper airplanes, and then dropped them off the top of the sliding board to see if they'd fly. Variables were tested through all kinds of fun experiments. We had nature hikes, planted a garden, exploded volcanoes in the classroom, and dissected frogs and owl pellets. My students and I made art collages from electronic equipment that we had torn apart while looking for simple machines. Every day, the students examined a slide under an electronic microscope and had to guess what it was. The winner had no homework that night. We wrote poetry and authored books. I say "we" because I normally participated with my students in all the activities. "Beat the Teacher" challenges were held to make as many words as possible from the letters of a selected word on the chalkboard. Yep, we still used blackboards and chalk back then. Teaching was pure fun. Years later, when standardized testing became the end-all, it was like the air escaped from our balloons. It just wasn't much fun anymore. I'm not so sure I would choose the same career if given another chance.

I was at Charles Dickens just two short years before I became pregnant with my daughter. At that time, I took a non-paid, two-year maternity leave, which was acceptable in those days. During those two years I gave birth to my daughter and then my son. Sadly, I experienced my first lay off from the Cleveland Schools, just when I was ready to return.

I taught in the Hough area in the Cleveland Public Schools for most of my twenty-five-year career. That included all subjects in grades three through eight. More than half of my career was dedicated to teaching adolescents. It was such a difficult world to be stuck in. Our students were able to go through their metamorphoses and grow out of that stage, but an adult who taught those grades, was caught in that web of raging hormones and sarcasm much too long.

Nathan Hale was my second school. I started there in 1978, after my first lay off experience. This time, I was there for three years before being laid off again. Cleveland Schools just didn't have the money to pay all of the teachers. Staffing adjustments were often made after the official student enrollment numbers came out during the month of October. That's when most of the laid off workers were called back to work.

During the 1970's, corporal punishment was the norm. I remember my first day walking into the junior high school for my next assignment. Nearly every adult was carrying a long, thick board. I had no idea what I was seeing. It turned out that the teachers were all ready to swat any students who weren't following the rules. I am ashamed to admit I quickly developed an excellent backhand; one that even the toughest students disliked. It wasn't totally unheard of that many students were also quite physical. My worse teaching experience was probably when an eighth grader punched me full force in the jaw in front of my entire class. He received a ten-day suspension, but then came right back to my classroom. That was at Nathan Hale, which was also known as Nathan Jail. More than a few of the students were very difficult there. But they weren't as bad as some of their parents who attacked the teachers, and defended their children, no matter what!

In all, I taught at four different Cleveland schools, was laid off twice, and survived three union strikes. One of those strikes happened to be the worst ever. It lasted nearly ten weeks and coincided with my separation and divorce period. At Nathan Hale, I reported to picket duty nearly every single day on crutches. Oh yeah, I forgot, I also had a broken leg then. I had fallen down the steps at school, while wearing clogs, on the very first day of our legal separation.

I believe the strike and picket line actually helped save my sanity. We met daily around an oil drum fire and roasted hotdogs and marshmallows. I had tremendous love and support from my colleagues, while trying to handle my divorce and my first strike simultaneously. I recall attempting to tutor a student on the picket line and was thoroughly discouraged from do-ing so. They taught me well. Michael and Marge, Al and Karen, Clarence, and Rosie were my best buds from Nathan Hale. We remain good friends today. That difficult teacher strike lasted October through December. My divorce was December 20, 1979, the day before my twenty-ninth birthday. The judge even peered over his glasses and wished me a "Happy Birth-day!" After my divorce, Clarence and I dated discreetly for about fifteen years, off and on. He always wanted to keep our relationship a secret. I was never comfortable with that because it seemed like he was ashamed of me. It took me a very long time to end that one, but I did break up with him.

My third school was a new magnet school, a direct result of the Fed-eral Desegregation Court order. Then, The Fundamental Education Center (F.E.C.) housed students in grades 1–8. I had an eighth-grade class that was the second most favorite group of my career. Those kids looked like adults, and I was one of the shortest people in the class. Eddie was the tallest at six feet, three inches. It was so strange after teaching at Nathan Hale. This was considered a Back-to-Basics school with strict rules. It had a dress code of navy-blue pants or skirts and solid white or light blue shirts, street shoes, and ties. Many staff members wore navy blue and white with tabards. F.E.C. was the first Cleveland Public School to man-date a uniform-like dress code.

This school was pretty much the opposite of Nathan Hale. My new principal confiscated my Cedar Point paddle that I had turned into a Hall Pass because she said it sent the wrong message. No corporal punishment was issued in this school. Eighth graders were treated just the same as the first graders. They marched in single file silent lines while walking in the halls to the restroom or the cafeteria. It was the only one of its kind in the Cleveland School System. Students were self-contained in one classroom most of the day. Really, it was run a lot like a parochial school.

I started there in 1981, one month after the school year began. I had been laid off for the second time and was getting pretty frustrated. However, I finally had enough seniority so I would not see another layoff. The first day, I gained the instant respect of my eighth graders and had no problems after that. I had to take my group down to the gym and teach them physical education class. So, I grabbed a basketball and challenged Eddie, the tallest kid to a free throw contest. The winner would be the first one to make a free throw shot. If the students won, there would be no homework for an entire week. If I won, they had to immediately quiet down each time I held my hand up. We all agreed. Eddie missed his first shot. I stood at the line, tossed that ball underhand, and SWISH, a perfect basket! I really don't know how it happened, but I had their attention from then on. I loved that group of students.

That same adolescent class caused a great deal of angst in my principal. They had to perform on stage for a spring assembly. I chose a fitness theme. They exercised to Olivia Newton John's "Let's Get Physical." My boss was terrified when the music started, but when she realized they would be doing jumping jacks, skipping rope, and touching their toes, she eased up. She later told me she had no idea where those eighth graders were headed with that song.

I was at F.E.C. for a total of 19 years, the biggest part of my teaching career. That's where I met some dear friends. Nancy, Donna, Jane, Janet, Wynnie, Ma Bea, and Joyce were among them. Joyce died way too soon from diabetes and heart problems. Also, after a few years there, my new boss was Leonard Steiger. Small world: Mr. Steiger had been my fourth-grade teacher at Dawning Elementary for one semester. He was well-respected and the best boss I ever worked for. He stayed at F.E.C. many years, before retiring.

Two of my biggest success stories at The Fundamental Education Center were significant accomplishments. The first was when a small group of my close teaching colleagues and I, worked hard to develop a grant proposal for technical classroom equipment. Our proposal for $250,000 was accepted, and we were able to put one desktop computer and software into each classroom. I know that doesn't sound like much, but it was then. Most schools had no computers at the time. Teachers developed rotating schedules to make sure every student was able to work on the computer. It was an exciting time for our school.

My other big school success was when I developed a Right-to-Read Celebration Sleepover. I had volunteered at Lyndie and G.J.'s school sleepover the year before and wanted to bring that kind of fun to my students. It took a great deal of planning, adult participants, donations, and patience. Finally, we received approval from the Board of Education to host the event. Teachers and other staff members gave up part of their weekend to stay overnight after working all week long. We had off-duty Cleveland police officers to provide security. Community members came to teach various lessons in their own areas of expertise. The local councilwoman showed up to read a bedtime story to the kids. Students participated in various activities and classes. Every hour was silent reading where students were supplied with free books. Teachers read bedtime stories to over 100 students in sleeping bags in the gym. It was well-planned and a tremendous success. We were able to repeat the program for the next several years.

Then, in 1996, Nancy and I had the opportunity to work as Peer Advisors for two years. We traveled to schools across the city each day to help new teachers get their feet on the ground. Beginning teachers tend to be thrown to the wolves. It's kind of a sink-or-swim mentality. Nearly half of the new teachers quit in their first five years. Our jobs were to assist them in methodology, planning, and execution of good lessons. In addition, we were to assist in discipline techniques. As peer advisors we observed and formally evaluated those teachers. We were the ones who ultimately decided if they would remain in the classroom or be terminated. Our evaluations of those teachers carried a great deal of weight in that decision.

One of the toughest tasks of my job was to fire someone. This teacher was an older gentleman, who happened to have been a very successful attorney. He wanted to give back to the community and chose to be a classroom teacher to do so. It just didn't work. The poor guy had absolutely zero discipline in that classroom. I tried everything to help him out. To me, classroom management, or discipline, is innate. It cannot be taught. Sure, some techniques make it a little better, but either you have it or you don't. That classroom was unsafe for him and his adolescent students. They broke the handle off his door and threw a desk, two chairs, and several books out the window, minutes before I showed up for his evaluation. It was a difficult choice to fire someone, but his teaching contract was definitely not renewed.

One extremely enjoyable part of that job was that Nancy and I also trained and became recruiters for the school district. Some of us peer advisors could opt to recruit, in addition to performing our other responsibilities. We were able to travel to various cities and states looking for new teachers who wanted to work in Cleveland. It was a learning opportunity and great fun traveling with my friend.

After that two-year assignment as a peer advisor, I made the mistake of returning to the classroom at my former school. Not long afterwards, my principal and I clashed. Prior to my peer advising assignment, she was my friend, and then as I was completing my Ph.D., I was suddenly her targeted enemy. I had asked questions on my doctoral survey regarding teachers witnessing any "cheating' behaviors on the part of colleagues or administrators. Perhaps her conscience was bothering her. Maybe she was worried about what would be discovered in her own school building. I really don't know what snapped in her, but she went through a complete change. The woman seemed to be mentally unstable. She sat outside my classroom each day, mornings, and afternoons, in a little first-grade desk and chair to harass me. I ignored her and left the door open continuing to teach hard, just as I always had. She claimed she was "docamenting" (She couldn't speak properly!), trying to catch me doing something. I have no idea what it was, but she never did catch me. And my way of coping with her harassment was to take the next day off work, every single time she made any derogatory comments to me. I usually had perfect attendance for the entire year and had accumulated well over 100 sick days. Not that year! I missed something like 17 days! They were necessary mental health days. That woman never did see the obvious direct relationship between my taking a day off and her harassment of me.

After putting up with her bullying for about six months, one day at a faculty meeting, I had taken all I was willing to take from her. I called her out. The principal was doing one of those blanket-blaming things, scolding the entire staff. She claimed: "Not one of you helped out. Not one of you lifted a finger to assist your colleagues." She was talking about a jump rope activity in the gym and ranted on and on, but it just wasn't true. I yelled out: "That's a lie!" She was telling a lie. Several of us had offered help during our planning time. The woman became furious and claimed I was insubordinate. She attempted to exert her authority and screamed that she could have me removed from the room. I told her to go right ahead. She didn't.

This went on for a bit and then the coup de grace! Under new business during that same meeting, my colleagues publicly recognized that I had completed my doctorate just a few days prior. They gave me a standing ovation, pulled out a big cake, and made a huge fuss. Unexpectedly, they sang "For She's a Jolly Good Fellow!" I think they were applauding more than just my doctorate; I had publicly stood up to that dictator.

The woman was so angry. Of course, I was written up because she wanted me fired. Meanwhile, I had been selected to present my Doctoral Dissertation findings at a research convention in Quebec. She refused to sign that permission paper. My original work had been published in a research journal and my name was already on the agenda. I had prepaid for my flight and my hotel room. There was no way she was keeping me from attending. So, I went anyway and called in sick. The principal tried to get me on "abusing sick leave" along with the "insubordination" charge. Eventually, I had a formal hearing downtown with a board member, the union attorney, my union rep, the district superintendent, and that crazy principal.

To begin the hearing, the superintendent pulled out a huge stack of papers. He read the top five or six of them aloud. Someone had started a writing campaign on my behalf. People from across the city wrote character witness letters for me attesting to my professionalism and teaching ability. There were more than fifty letters from my past and present colleagues, my peer advisees and other advisors, my former principals, secretarial and custodial staff members, and professors from Cleveland State, all supporting me. The superintendent gave me the letters. I was overwhelmed with emotion, but held it in. I felt extremely fortunate to have so many people stand up for me when I really needed help. Bottom line, that principal should have stayed home on that particular day! I won the entire hearing, and she was humiliated. For the next two months she didn't say another word to me, until evaluation time.

At the end of the school year, that principal had to call me in for a formal evaluation. Of course, I had all "Excellent" marks until that point for many, many years; including those I had received from her! This time, to make herself feel better, she just had to give me one "Unsatisfactory." The derogatory mark was under "Knowledge of Subject," of all things! Like

I didn't know the third-grade curriculum! However, I got the last word in. I turned to leave, and she said, "Ms. Wyman," I interrupted her and said, "That's Dr. Wyman to you!" as I turned on my heal and abruptly walked out. I didn't have to listen to anything else that woman had to say. I think I grinned for an entire week after that incident! And then just to rub it in, I wore my doctoral cap and gown for the formal class picture with my students. I hope she enjoyed her copy of that photo!

I put in a transfer request, as did several other teachers. I ended up teaching just one year at Martin Luther King Jr. Law and Public Service Magnet School. It was a tough school, but I was happy and well respected where my new boss called me Doc. And that crazy former principal was fired at the end of the next year. Poetic justice does exist.

Chapter 19

My Travels

The more you read the more things you'll know.
The more you learn, the more places you'll go.
~Dr. Seuss~

Traveling has been something I have always enjoyed. Sometimes I traveled with family, colleagues, a new group, or alone. I have enjoyed the ocean and beaches in numerous Caribbean islands, Mexico, Florida, and Bermuda. Some of my most interesting trips were to New Orleans, nearly all Canadian provinces, and Poland. Only in the past few years, have I seen California, specifically, the Pacific Ocean and the mountains of Yosemite National Park.

My most extreme trip was to Poland. A teaching colleague, Ma Bea, and I had signed up for an Alaskan cruise. She changed her mind and convinced me to travel to Krakow, Poland to teach English to Polish high school students. I agreed. Then Ma Bea changed her mind again and I went without her. A group of educators from the Cleveland area traveled together, so I made new friends. What an experience!

It was 1989 and Poland was still a Communist country. Our students were extremely respectful and eager to learn English. It was so enjoyable because we were there simply to let them hear and practice American English. Good thing because I didn't understand or speak Polish. I knew "pierogies and kielbasa," but that was about it. Most of our lessons centered around conversations, idioms, and lyrics to popular American songs.

The Polish students loved songs like Billy Joel's "I Didn't Start the Fire", Paula Abdul's hit "Straight Up", and "If You Don't Know Me by Now" from Simply Red. They especially liked slower songs that made it a little easier to hear the words clearly. But one of their favorite songs was "Take Me Out to the Ballgame." We lived in a dormitory at the historic Jagiellonian University with students from all over the world. It was not unusual to hear four or five different languages spoken at the breakfast table.

Upon arrival I mistakenly saw the city as drab and poor. I was ignorant of history. In fact, the buildings were thousands of years old and surrounded by medieval walls. The Sukiennice, a 14th Century Cloth Hall, was in the center of Krakow. I had nothing to compare it to, seeing as The United States was only 200 years old! These buildings were made of natural stone, not painted bright colors. Krakow, Poland was filled with historic architecture and culture. It was completely like stepping back in time. There were one-horse pull carts on the street. Women in babushkas swept sidewalks with homemade brooms. People swatted flies off their cows or beat rugs with long hand-woven wooden paddles. Many Poles seemed to push start their small cars. Shopping supplies were extremely limited, and every item was behind a counter, which made it difficult when we were unable to speak the language. Many times, our students accompanied us to the market, so they could translate. It was great practice for them and they rescued their American teachers, or professors, as they called us.

What I found most difficult about the Poland trip was it was a very hot summer and good clean drinking water just didn't exist. We lined up to get water from wells, but that was awful. We purchased refilled brown bottles, but more than once we found worms at the bottom or some strange oil floating on top. Sometimes, we walked to the nearest hotel and bought a glass of ice water. I was constantly thirsty.

Teachers and students went on many trips. We experienced the solemn reality of two Concentration Camps, Auschwitz and Sobibor. We attended bonfires in the Niepołomnicka Forest, went white water rafting on the Dunajec River, and sang lyrics from the *Sound of Music* and the *Wizard of Oz*, at the top of our lungs in the beautiful mountain town of Zakopane. We toured Wawel Castle, gilded Catholic churches, and amazing museums. One especially memorable excursion was to the great Wieliczka Salt Mine. It was like an entire underground city that included rivers, statues, chapels, and amazingly, a health resort. Our students told us that some of them with breathing issues had to live in the salt mine after the Chernobyl explosion. We enjoyed students singing Toto's "Africa" atop the mountain in cable cars. We taught the young teens to play baseball and how to celebrate the Halloween holiday. Our group of American teachers had fun wherever we went, and whatever we did with those students.

Ironically, one of the funniest things that happened to me in Poland, was when we visited the Tomb of the Unknown Soldier in Warsaw. Because Poland was ruled under a Communist government, we had been warned not to photograph Russian soldiers, bridges, or railways. At the Tomb, two Russian soldiers marched back and forth. I had my huge over-the-shoulder camcorder. When they had their backs to me, I decided to break the rule. I started videoing the soldiers marching. Without warning, they suddenly clicked their heels together, turned, pointed their rifles, and marched directly toward me. I almost died! I dropped my camera and quickly stepped backwards. My friend fell to the ground, laughing so hard she nearly peed her pants. The soldiers chuckled and kept marching past us. What I didn't know was that at that exact second, their precise marching routine demanded a quick about-face. The joke was on me. Reviewing the video, you can clearly hear me cry, "Oh shit!" as the movie suddenly goes black.

I loved the Poland experience so much that I went back for a second teaching assignment the next year. That time, I took my 14-year-old son with me. The students all loved G.J. and interacted positively with him. He lived with the school principal, her husband, and their 16-year-old son, who was one of my students. They spoke only Russian in the home and no one in the family spoke English. The two boys carried their Polish-English dictionaries everywhere they went. G.J. had a lifetime of Polish history, vocabulary, and culture all in one summer. He was very happy to get off the plane when we arrived back home. G.J. literally got down on his knees and bowed to the ground.

CHAPTER 20

An Accident in Bermuda

You will face many defeats in life,
but never let yourself be defeated.
~Maya Angelou~

My sister Fran, lived in Bermuda for more than 25 years. I was quite envious of her life because she was living my dream, right on the water. Fortunately, she allowed me to visit her in Bermuda too many times to count. My last trip to Bermuda in June 2000, changed my entire life in mere seconds. I had just completed my Ph.D. the year before, but that year I taught summer school. For the first time in at least 10 years I was going to spend the entire summer doing only what I chose to do. There was to be no work, no studying, no writing: just pure fun for two months! Unfortunately, I was dealt the wrong cards for that kind of summer.

In Bermuda, I always drove a moped, which was the typical method of transportation. At that time, there were no rental cars on the tiny 22 square mile island. I had just left the beach and came out of the grocery store parking lot. Within seconds after buckling my helmet and pulling out onto the main road, I jackknifed the scooter and flipped over the handlebars, landing on my left shoulder. The moped whipped around and smashed my leg. A very small child stood right over me in the middle of the street and was staring into my pained face, as I screamed in agony. I asked the firefighters to move him away and wondered where his parents were. When I was transported into an ambulance, I saw one of my favorite things, a beautiful rainbow, and thought I was going to die. I ended up in the hospital for a week with surgery on my leg, which was broken in three places. They put a long rod, screws, and pins in it. The shoulder was crushed in five places and dislocated. I really didn't like that Bermuda Hospital's ER staff. Several of the professionals attending to my severe situation seemed to lack the TLC usually found in nurses back home. I was actually yelled at more than once for screaming out in such agonizing pain. They said I was disturbing the other patients. They also yelled at me because my left arm and shoulder were in such an awkward position. They wanted to know who put my arm like that. According to the doctors, the broken shoulder was too complicated for them to operate on in Bermuda. After a week in the hospital, I stayed another week in a private home with Fran's mother-in-law, Bobbie. She took great care of me. Then I flew home strapped in, kind of like Hannibal Lecter in *Silence of the Lambs*, minus the mask.

Once I arrived in Cleveland, my doctoral cohort friend, Vida, met me on the plane with a wheelchair. I was in good hands with Vida because she was a nurse and made sure I was safe. In this smashed up condition, I stayed with my dear friends and next-door neighbors, Nancy and Donna for about three weeks. I was in horrific pain, but they made me laugh every single day. I couldn't have asked for better caregivers. They administered my daily shots and meds, took me to all appointments, prepared my meals, did my laundry, paid my bills, and took care of Arlo, my dog.

I was in a wheelchair with very limited abilities. I laugh now as I recall how we first made Donna attempt to do every task before I tried them. She could only use her right arm and leg, so she simulated my condition. Poor Donna had to get up and down from the toilet, step in and out of the shower, feed herself, pour beverages, brush her teeth, wash and comb her hair, and anything else you can imagine, right-sided only. My pain level was greater than 99 out of 10, so I couldn't fathom doing anything that would cause me more pain. Donna was such a good sport, and oh so funny, but more importantly, she helped me to see what I should or should not attempt to do alone. Donna and Nancy held a daily competition to see who could take the best care of me. They both did, so I was the clear winner! I could not have made it without their help.

Nearly six weeks after the accident, and various doctors, I ended up with a total shoulder replacement and serious nerve damage. The nerves had been wound around the ball and socket of the humerus all those weeks. I was in two hospitals and a nursing home for four full months. I do have a permanent nerve condition from the damage. It's called RSD, or reflex sympathetic dystrophy. That name has since been changed to CRPS, or complex regional pain syndrome. Basically, it means I have a life of chronic pain, while my body is continually in fright-flight mode. With certain limitations, I am still able to function and enjoy life. Pain, a nerve condition, and range of motion tend to be my biggest obstacles.

The nursing home I was in for rehabilitation was Judson Park. I was in very bad shape when I entered, but the staff took great care of me. I was in and out of the hospital and back to the nursing home a few times, but the most compassionate care I received was from the therapists at Judson. I did therapy for many hours, twice daily. Over time, I was able to swim one-armed laps in their therapeutic swimming pool. My teaching career was over as soon as I crashed that moped. The Judson staff's hard work and dedication impressed me so much, that I decided to volunteer there weekly for the next ten years. I developed some very lasting friendships at Judson during that period. Bogusia, Susan, Clyde, and Sharon are still my friends today, 22 years later. Eventually, I stopped volunteering when I moved forty minutes away and it got to be too much traveling.

Meanwhile, I also began to work with another therapist, Josh. I met him at an outpatient facility. Shortly after we started working together, he opened his own business specializing in a streamlined personal training experience. Now, Christina is my trainer there. We get along extremely well because she has a great sense of humor; yet she pushes me hard so I don't lose strength or mobility.

CHAPTER 21

My Grandkids

Only through love will we find our way to create a world
worthy of our children and our grandchildren.
~Laurence Overmire~

I cannot believe I have eight grandkids! I love them dearly and appreciate all their unique qualities and characteristics. The COVID Pandemic has certainly impacted the relationship I have with my grandchildren. I miss them and it's sad because they are full of joy and bring such hope into this world. I love when I can spend time with them.

My daughter, Lyndie, and my son-in-law, Rocky, have three teenagers and live fairly close to me. They're excellent parents who are extremely involved in the lives of their kids. The parents have provided a beautiful, safe, loving, nurturing environment for their children. Lyndie is an educator, like her momma. She is a guidance counselor in Lakewood Schools and also a school board member for Cuyahoga Heights District. Rocky is a very successful businessman. He is the co-owner of a construction company that builds and remodels homes.

Their treehouse, trampoline, pool, and gigantic yard are favorite hangouts for all the neighborhood kids. Lyndie and Rocky are very real and honest with their children. The kids come first and always have. Both parents attend all school and sporting events involving each of their children. Volunteering at school and community activities takes up a good deal of their time. Both Lyndie and Rocky have coached numerous sports for kids in the village of Brooklyn Heights. They travel to various cities and states for their kids' sport teams and take them on great vacations. They have even gone on a family cruise. Lyndie and Rocky are hands-on parents who provide everything their kids could need or want.

I had the privilege of watching those three teenagers way back when they were babies and toddlers, until all three kids were in school. I was exhausted when I babysat full-time all those years, but I truly loved it. I felt very close to Lyndie's kids. We baked gluten-free cookies and made GA-GA's chicken. The kids and I read daily, created cities with cars and blocks, painted, crafted, and often went to the Natural History Museum. We loved taking a trip to Sweeties Candy Shop or Honey Hut Ice Cream. We played endless board games, which Cole regularly seemed to win. Word of caution; he does tend to cheat!

My favorite game to play with them was "Guess How Much Money is in GA-GA's Wallet!" If anyone guessed the right amount, they got to keep it. Tegan was the first winner with $128! I made her buy each of her brothers something. Right away I realized how expensive the game could be, so we all agreed to put a cap on it. The correct guesser would always tie Tegan's winnings. Months later, Cole was the next winner. He often was the closest to the exact number, even if he didn't win. If someone won a second time, they just got $20. We are still waiting for poor Owen to win. He is usually nowhere close. However, he was only $4 off on his last guess.

OWEN is my oldest grandchild. He is responsible for naming me GA-GA, the name that all my grandkids call me. I was going to be called "Granny." Everyday Owen would turn to me and ask, "Where Momma go?" "Where Dada go?" I usually responded with, "They went to work." One day I pointed to myself and said, "Owen, who is here?" He tried to say "Granny" but said "GA-GA." That's been my name ever since, and I love it!

When Owen was very young, like one and two years old, he was fascinated by vacuum cleaners. That boy knew how to identify all the popular brands just by looking at pictures of them. He loved to sit and find the cleaning tools in catalogues and newspaper ads. When his family went to visit people, it was the norm for Owen to go directly to their closets to search for vacuums. If he couldn't find one, he'd ask, "What do you have? A Hoover or a Bissell? Or do you have a Dirt Devil?" Owen was beyond thrilled when I let him pick out my new vacuum at Target. He chose a red Dirt Devil. That toddler loved to clean and wasn't at all worried that the machine was so loud or double his height. He spent hours pushing vacuums around, plugged or unplugged. He loved to unwind and rewind the long cords. I wrote a book for Owen about his love of vacuum cleaners.

Owen is a bright, sweet, kind, sensitive eighteen-year-old. He has some qualities that I sincerely respect. From a very young age Owen has been terrific with babies and little kids. We called him "The Baby Whisperer." He was so natural in gaining their attention, calming them down, or making them smile. In that respect, Owen is a lot like his dad and his uncles. Rocky, G.J., Jimmy, and Mackey are good family male role-models. They're all great with kids; that is, when they aren't accidentally bumping their heads on the ceiling. Owen is excellent with his little cousins, and extremely patient, even when they try to annoy him.

The second quality I admire in Owen is his ability to hold adult-like discussions. I love when we sit and chat about anything and everything. You never have to water down any conversations with him. Owen has always been able to have lengthy discussions on a very mature level. He listens and engages whomever he is speaking with. Even his school superintendent loves having private chats with Owen, who stops into his office to do well-checks on the head of the school system. I love that!

And perhaps his most important admirable quality, is Owen's determination or dedication. When he sets goals, like being a football kicker, nothing stops him. He learns everything he possibly can, and then does whatever it takes to make that a reality.

Owen just finished his senior year at Cuyahoga Heights High School. He and his girlfriend, Bella, went to two proms because she is from another school. Owen has already graduated and is off to college in the fall. He will attend John Carroll University, which is nice because it's just outside of Cleveland. His Uncle Mike was a student there. Owen is extremely talented in his chosen sport, football. He has had a very exciting and successful kicking career so far. We look forward to seeing some great things come from this young man; athletically, and more importantly, academically.

TEGAN is just 16 months younger than Owen. At age sixteen, she completed the tenth grade and had a fun year. Her braces came off, she began dating, received her driver's license, and started her first job as a server at Aladdin's restaurant. She is sharp as a whip with an acute sense of humor. Tegan is extremely intelligent, and her logical mind leaves amateur debaters in the dust. She has always been a Daddy's Girl and has had Rocky wrapped around her little finger. I think he knows she manipulates him, but he doesn't mind.

When I babysat for Tegan, I loved seeing what outfit she had selected each day. She created her own ensemble and had a style like no other child. She wore things like a ruffled rainbow dress with two different patterned knee socks, an oversized bright t-shirt, and a stuffed animal on her head. Tegs always loved bright colors! At a very young age, her favorite color was magenta. She was sure to correct people when they called it red or pink. When she was little, Tegan had the cutest hot pink cowgirl boots and hats. Lots of hats because that baby girl loved her hats. The book

I wrote for Tegan was all about her hats. It was easy to obtain numerous photos because she loved posing in her hats. And the sillier, the better.

Tegan is absolutely stunning, with dark hair, dark eyes, and a beautiful smile. She has many talents and will develop new ones as she continues to learn more about herself. Tegs is athletic and currently plays on a traveling volleyball team. She was also on the Cuyahoga Heights track team, where she jumped hurdles for a bit, until she was injured. Art has been a long-time interest of hers since she was a toddler. Tegan loves to paint and tends to see beauty where others may not. I swear her eyes notice colors and shapes differently than the rest of us. I am excited to imagine the doors that will open to Tegan's bright future.

COLE is currently thirteen and completed eighth grade. He is quick, impish, and undoubtedly the funniest guy in the family. Cole's number one interest is sports. Since he was very little, he was telling the refs or umpires how to do their jobs. He is serious about whatever sport he plays. He watches everything and takes it all in. In fact, as early as flag football, Cole was tackling everyone because that's what he had observed from watching the pros. He is THE most dedicated Browns fan I have ever known. When the Browns lost every single game in the season, Cole didn't give up on them.

One of Cole's favorite things to do is to help his parents host the treehouse parties for friends when the Browns play. He looks forward to these parties every weekend because of the delicious tailgate cuisine, outdoor games, and endless fun. In spite of having COVID in December, Cole wrapped himself in blankets and sat outside on the deck, peering in through the big windows to watch the Browns game in the living room.

Cole has asthma and severe allergies to dogs. We found that out many years ago when he immediately broke out in hives and his eyes swelled shut the last time he was near my dog. Tegan was also diagnosed with asthma but seems fine with dogs. Cole has had reactions to dogs and oak at various times since. So, we don't take any chances with my dog. It seems the labs have a certain type of dander that Cole cannot tolerate. The kids almost never come to my house.

Cole is very bright, but chooses when, where, and how to apply himself. I think he may one day end up being the wealthiest kid in the family. He is clever and quick with numbers or money. He already knows how to make a fast buck. For example, when the school recently changed its name from the Redskins to the Red Wolves the superintendent gave all students new t-shirts. Cole immediately turned around and sold his shirt to an upperclassman. Cole can accomplish great things, but sometimes gets frustrated along the way. He can be a handful, but also quite loving and affectionate.

Cole has a very sweet side and can be generous. I remember when he was just in preschool, his favorite game was "Uno-Moo." On his teacher's birthday, he wrapped his game in newspaper and Band-Aids and gave it to her as a gift. He was very upset that she didn't return it, so I had to go out and buy him another one. Cole's gift to his teacher was an extremely generous act because he loved that game; almost as much as he loved sticking me with the "Old Maid" in another game.

Garbage Day was Cole's favorite holiday! From the time he was a young toddler, he was infatuated with big trucks. No matter where he was, or what he was doing, if he heard those squeaky brakes, even two or three blocks away, Cole ran to the door or window to watch for the garbage trucks. He often stood out at the curb, sometimes in just a diaper, to supervise the pickup and dumping process. Cole took his neighbor, Mary's, trash out with her weekly. He gathered up twigs just so he would have something to put in the cans. He loved to haul his family's full, heavy trash containers out to the curb and line them up just perfectly. The collection crews got to know Cole and fondly talked to him each week. One time, they lifted him and let him pull the lever to compress the trash in the back end of the huge truck. Cole was ecstatic! Then he would take all the cans back to the yard. Sometimes, he was upset with his Uncle John's family next-door because they often took their own trash cans in and out. Cole's book from me was obviously about his garbage truck obsession. To his surprise, it included a British garbage truck photo that his cousin, Kirsten, sent from London.

Coleman loves attention and makes friends easily. He knows exactly how to entertain people. Cole's sense of humor is sharper than most kids his age. He loves photo bombing pictures when his brother or sister are all dressed up for formal dances. Most of their friends love Cole. I can't wait to see his journey through maturity. I just hope his teachers have an equally great sense of humor.

Then, there are my five **TAMPA BABIES**. However, they aren't babies anymore, and they no longer live in Tampa. Allison, my-daughter-in-law, and my son, G.J., have five children. They lived in Tampa for eight years, but now live in Bradenton, Florida. They are also excellent parents. With five kids born like steps, these two must have the patience of saints. It is obvious that their kids come first in all of their decisions and choices. Like Lyndie and Rocky, they hold down full-time careers. Allison is a surgeon and G.J. is a physical therapist. They employ an au pair to get some help. Both Allison and G.J. are involved in every part of their kids' lives. It is clear how much love is in their family. The kids enjoy a beautiful, luxurious, safe setting and the adornment from both parents. I have decided my son is like a private amusement park ride for his kids. He just loves to play with them. Sometimes I believe Allison has six kids!

Allison and G. take the kids on regular outings as often as possible. They go to water parks, the zoo, around the block in their "wagon train", take bike rides, go on the pontoon boat and raft, swim in their pool, or play at the beach condo. They enjoy spending weekends away, camping in their RV. They make sure the kids are getting real life learning experiences. Although they live so far away, they make a conscious effort to stay connected with their Ohio families via FaceTime, phone calls, texting, and numerous trips. Unfortunately, I do not see these Florida babies often, but I genuinely love them with all my heart. I just wish I knew more about their individual characteristics or what makes them tick.

EMERY is the oldest Florida grandchild, at age nine. She'll start the fourth grade soon. I feel like I know a little bit more about Em than her siblings because I spent more time with her. When Em was a baby, Allison and G.J. brought her to Lyndie's house so I could watch her with Cole, while Owen and Tegan were in school most of the day. Emery is like Cole in some ways. She is very funny and likes to laugh and joke around. Learning is fairly easy, as Emery is quite clever. She is also gorgeous and is starting to look very much like her momma. Since she was a baby, Emery has had a smile that could instantly light up a room. Emery is probably the best big sister I have ever known. She recently told me she wants to babysit for her first job. She certainly has experience along that line. With four little brothers, she is kind, patient, and a good role-model. Of course, there are times when Ms. Em needs attention, but for the most part, she is very well-behaved. She helps the little ones and has a good sense of safety and accident prevention. Perhaps when she is a teenager, Emery will be tired of being surrounded by four brothers, but for right now she holds her own. Whatever she chooses to do when she grows up, I believe Ms. Em will make a difference in this world.

DANE is the oldest boy in the Florida bunch. For a long time, he appeared to be his daddy's clone. Young Dane's pictures were almost identical to his father's childhood photos. He is currently eight years old and can be a handful at times. On other occasions, like one-on-one, Dane is fun, loving, and inquisitive. Sometimes he demands attention, both good and bad, and does whatever it takes to receive it. Dane will be going into grade three next school year. He gets bored with rules and regulations, and just wants to be on his own exploring and getting into things. He lifts rocks, turns wheels, takes things apart, and examines the most intricate details. His very intelligent, inquisitive mind may lead him to a fascinating profession. Dane's interests and his need to explore objects could prove useful someday, but in school he is often unable to investigate at will. Right now, he is working on reining it in. Maybe those gorgeous puppy dog eyes will help to keep him out of trouble. I love talking to Dane on the phone. He is very well-spoken and sounds so mature. I would not be surprised if Dane becomes a very successful engineer one day.

CADE is definitely a middle child. He is six years old and has completed kindergarten. Cade is the one family member who most resembles his momma's side of the family. He looks very much like his Papa Miketa and his Uncle Aaron, Allison's brother. Cade is a people pleaser and is doing well in school. He likes learning and is often happy off by himself just doing his own thing. Cade seems to be a little accident prone. Perhaps a better way to say that is Cade isn't afraid of much. He is willing to try new things without worrying too much about the physical consequences. Part of that is he just wants to do whatever his older sibs are doing. He doesn't want to be seen as one of the babies. At this early age, Cade goes through his share of bleeding and Band-Aids. But he doesn't let any injury stop him from trying again. I admire that quality in Cade. He's a tough little dude, and likely, that will help him achieve future success.

ROCCO, who is pure cuteness, just had his fifth birthday. He's a little shy around me, so I don't know him well. Rocco has a great disposition and is usually very happy. He has the cutest little smile, especially when he is up to mischief. He enjoys playing with his siblings things when they aren't around. It's not unusual to spot Rocco contentedly playing by himself with his toys. He also loves to interact with his brothers and sister and enjoys following their lead. He is just sweet. Rocco is the only one who has an opportunity to go to school this summer. He is extremely excited and loves learning. Watching Rocco grow into his own will be a fun journey.

ELI is last (for now anyhow), but not least. He is our dear, adorable little guy who just exudes happiness. His disposition is a great deal like that of Rocco. Like the old song says, "Eli's coming! Hide your heart girl!" He is beautiful! Eli is only two years old. His gorgeous eyes, long lashes, and blond hair make him so darn cute. The most I have gotten from Eli is a shy thigh hug, but I'll take it. He does talk to me on the phone when we FaceTime, but he especially loves to see my dog, Clinton, or to look at my fish tank. Eli joins in on the family fun every chance he gets. He seems like a very happy little toddler and just tries to keep up with the older sibs. Hopefully, they will teach him a lot of good things. I wish that Eli's journey in life is pure fun and that he remains as happy as he is today.

So, each one of my eight grandkids is different from the other. That's what keeps it fresh. They are all unique characters and lots of fun. The only problem is they grow up way too fast! I love them all dearly and they give me hope for the future. The dysfunctional family cycle has been broken. My children and grandchildren all know, and experience, genuine love—as do I.

CHAPTER 22

Living on My Own

You must be the change you wish to see in the world.
~Gandhi~

Two months before our divorce was final, I left our brand-new house in Brooklyn Heights and moved to an apartment building in Parma. My stay in our new home had been less than seven months. I didn't have much choice, seeing as the house now belonged to Jim's father. Unbeknownst to me, Jim cunningly had me sign that new house over to his father while completing a stack of joint tax forms. He unexpectantly had his friend, Michael Grodach, there to witness the signatures. I remember thinking that it was quite odd that Michael signed our tax forms, but I was very young and naive. I'm sure Jim had that house back in his own name immediately following the dissolution of our marriage. Believe me, you never want to divorce a lawyer! Perhaps it's not a good idea to divorce a writer either.

Anyhow, remaining fairly close was important because there was a great deal of back and forth traveling in our joint custody arrangement. We shared the kids half-week. Joint custody was not at all common back then. Of course, I thought I'd never need it, but I had seen an episode explaining the process on the old talk show, *Phil Donahue*. Then, when I was faced with it, I thought joint custody would be the best solution to keep both parents equally involved in our kids' lives. In hindsight, I gave Jim too much power and I was much too accommodating regarding the kids. I wanted my children to experience the family concept that I never had, as much as possible, and I didn't believe I could provide that. There were no cousins, aunts, uncles, or grandparents on my side that they could spent quality time with. My sister, Fran, and their one cousin, Kirsten, were too far away, in Bermuda. At their father's they had four more siblings and an abundance of other relatives. I should have realized that we were a real family, just the three if us. I would definitely do it differently if I had another chance.

Next, I moved to Regency Towers at 6100 Laurent Dr. in Parma, Ohio. I loved that place! At that time it was a beautiful apartment complex but has seriously declined over the years. We had a rec center with a huge indoor pool. That's where both kids learned to swim. Lyndie, G.J., and I spent a great deal of time at that pool. On the fifth floor we had a two-bedroom and then, after a few years, we moved into a large three-bedroom apartment. I stayed there for ten years, driving to and from the east side every day for teaching.

In 1990, the same year I had taught in Poland and started my doctoral studies, I moved to 2832 Mayfield Road in Cleveland Heights. I had been to Nancy Tondy's master's degree party and saw the house next door for sale. Nancy and Donna were my teaching colleagues at the time, and we had become very close friends. When I toured the Mayfield Road house, I immediately fell in love with it, so I bought it! Unfortunately, I never had the time, energy, or funds to do much with it because of my studies. I did have a built-in screen porch with a sunken hot tub added onto the back of the house. That was my sanctuary. I couldn't live on the lake yet, so I brought the water to my own yard.

It was so much fun living next to Donna and Nancy. We had lengthy, entertaining conversations through our open windows. We took care of each other, as well as one another's pets. We had the same locks on our back door for two reasons. Donna and Nancy got locked out more than once, and it was a challenge to find a way in. Climbing on a ladder and pushing Donna through a window was one way to enter the house. The problem was, we could hardly succeed because we would laugh so hard. The other reason for the shared lock was so the first person to arrive home could let our dogs, Tucker and Arlo, or later, Jesse, outside.

Nancy seemed to be the most practical of the three of us. Donna and I were the problem solvers. We believed we could handle anything that was thrown our way. Nancy usually chose the most reasonable solution. When Donna and I came up with some crazy idea, Nancy would just shake her head and move on. Those two were the hardest working women I had ever known. Through painstaking effort and diligence, they made their home into a gorgeous showplace.

Their outside landscaping job was extremely laborious and it required truckloads of mulch. There was a cute little garden-like area up on top of a big hill in the backyard. The problem was transporting heavy buckets of mulch up the narrow steps. Nancy kept working while Donna and I cleverly devised a pulley system using the dog leads to get that mulch uphill. It didn't work! The very first bucket went up, up, up, and immediately back down, slamming into my Birkenstocked toes! It ripped my big toenail right off, the blood gushed out, and the toe was broken. That was one of our less successful problem-solving activities. Of course, we did eventually laugh about it.

We had a shared driveway, or I should say, ski slope. It was such a crazy hill! Winter was an absolute nightmare. When it snowed, we'd get stuck trying to get up, slide back down, and then have to reverse across the very busy Mayfield Road. Once traffic cleared, we had to push the pedal to the metal, and gun the engine all the way up the drive. Usually, it took several attempts, or we would get stuck sideways. I think that driveway was the only negative thing about my Mayfield Road house.

Autumn was gorgeous in that backyard, where we couldn't hear any of the busy Mayfield Road traffic. There were so many decades old giant oak, elm, and sycamore trees, and the fall colors were amazing. The hard part was keeping those leaves off the driveway, just like the snow and ice, so we could drive on it without skidding right onto Mayfield. Every fall, we spent many days cleaning up those leaves. We raked them into huge tarps and all three of us had to drag them down the driveway to the tree lawn. It took numerous trips over several days. Great exercise; greater teamwork.

My favorite next door neighbor story is when I taught Donna how to make a Thanksgiving turkey. Donna was kind of a germophobe and that was long before the COVID pandemic. She wore a head scarf, long rubber gloves, and an apron. Let's just say, she did not appreciate having to stick her hand up inside that turkey and pull out the innards. I could hardly breathe I was laughing so hard. It's difficult to do justice in trying to describe the scene, but it was definitely like something out of a *Mr. Bean* video. I think we may have even dropped the turkey on the floor, or we came very close to doing so. We constantly laughed, no matter what we did. However, Donna did learn how to make a delicious turkey. I was so proud of her.

I really loved living next to Nancy and Donna. We did so much together. We ate out or did take out from Little Italy. We walked on Coventry and enjoyed people-watching. Sometimes we hiked around on the big hills in scenic Lakeview Cemetery. The Cedar Lee Theater was nearby and we enjoyed seeing the foreign films, or smaller production movies. Often, we carpooled to work together. The three of us talked for hours on end about teaching, politics, families, movies, and travels. We just had fun. I lived there for 14 years, which, at that time, was the longest I had ever lived anywhere in my life. I was lucky to have such dear friends and neighbors. As an extra bonus, Nancy and Donna's best friends, Kim and Nancy, moved into a house right behind us. I had the chance to know and love them, too. They were also teachers and founded a very successful company called Simple Solutions and Bright Ideas Press. I was fortunate to work for them from home after my accident in Bermuda. I wrote Study Skills workbooks for students and was absolutely addicted to the research and writing process. It took my mind off of my chronic pain issues. I was forever grateful to them for giving me that wonderful opportunity.

Nancy and Kim were really quite talented at home repair and remodeling. They rebuilt my huge Mayfield Road kitchen with their own hands. They did a beautiful job, and the craftsmanship was impeccable.

I sadly moved on because I was babysitting my first grandson, Owen, full-time. It was so hard to leave those friends. However, the problem was, I lived in Cleveland Heights. Rocky and Lyndie were in Broadview Heights then, and Lyndie's job was in Lakewood. It wasn't working because we all spent way too much time on the road, especially on snowy days. So, G.J. bought my house and I bought a southwest side condo at 6488 State Road in Parma.

That's when I met my friend, Lori. At the time I bought my condo, I needed some help. My junior high pal, Chris, worked with Lori and introduced us. Now, seventeen years later, Lori and I are still friends. We have a lot in common and seriously enjoy our discussions. Lori is an amazing single mom, whom I honestly admire. She successfully raised two bright, beautiful young sons, Shane and Aaron. At times, she took on two or three jobs to make sure she could provide for her family. She is a hard-working educator in the Parma School System. And boy is she smart! I thought I was clever, but I never could beat Lori in Words with Friends! She has helped me out a great deal throughout the years. My dog, Clinton, loves her as much as he loves me. She is his surrogate mommy each time I go on vacation. I know my pup is in good hands and I never have to worry about leaving him. I am honestly grateful to have Lori in my life.

I liked being close to my daughter, Lyndie, as she also moved, this time to Brooklyn Heights. We were only about ten minutes apart then and it was much easier for babysitting. However, I hated Parma. Cleveland Heights had much more to offer in the way of culture, museums, unusual restaurants, and multiculturally diverse residents. Parma was solid white demographically, with limited independent eateries. It did have large Ukrainian and Polish populations that proudly celebrated their cultures and heritages.

I lucked out once again because I ended up living next door to a beautiful, loving Ukrainian family. For nearly fifteen years the Vilshanetskys and I were close friends. Olena and Oleh had two wonderful young daughters, Marta and Diana. I saw both of those girls turn into gorgeous, intelligent young adults. From the very beginning, when Marta was about eight years old, I watched her learn to swim when we went to our condo pool nearly every day in the summer. After swimming, we sat on a little wooden bench out front where we played checkers, did math problems, or read hours on end. Marta learned very quickly and took in everything I had to offer. Diana was only about two years old then and it was difficult to include her in our activities. Over the years, I watched Diana become an equally amazing young girl. She loved to go to my grandchildren's house with me, where she got along extremely well with those kids. They enjoyed teasing Diana endlessly, especially the youngest one, Cole.

Now Oleh and Olena have a third beautiful little toddler, Roxelana. Currently, Diana is a student at Cleveland State University. Marta graduated from the same school and was married in Ukraine less than a year ago. She is now collecting donations from all over the world to buy and deliver supplies to the Ukrainian soldiers during this horrible Russian invasion.

She is extremely brave! The Vilshanetskys were a beautiful family, and I was fortunate to live next to them for such a long time. They were sweet neighbors and I genuinely loved them.

My sister lived with me in Parma for most of those years. I was never happy and found it difficult to share my home with someone else after being on my own for so long. We had to cook and eat separately because of my celiac condition. It seemed like one of us was always waiting for the kitchen or the shower. We didn't do much together. Fran stayed in her bedroom whenever she wasn't working or cooking. She did have a job, but never helped with the bills. I was constantly resentful and felt used. It wasn't a good situation for either of us. It was time to sell the condo and just live in an apartment by myself.

I moved here to Berea Lakes Apartments in July 2018. I truly love it here because Berea has everything to offer. My new home is 144 Coe Street. Situated right on Coe Lake, my new apartment provides a breath-taking view of the water. That view changes hourly every day, every season. The wild animals like groundhogs, squirrels, deer, opossums, and racoons stop by for food several times a day. There are a variety of ducks, geese, herons, and other unlimited birds, in constant view. I have spotted a beautiful bald eagle on more than one occasion. I see all the activity from graduations, weddings, proms, and photo shoots right from my living room. I love watching the 70-foot fountain spraying water and dancing in the wind. Sometimes in the early morning a beautiful rainbow appears in the fountain mist. I can see fireworks and hear live concerts while sitting out on my patio. Horses trotting up and down my street never cease to amaze me. I love the smell of a fire in the pavilion's large fireplace right across the lake. It reminds me of my days at Hiram House Camp. I must admit, when I hear all the laughter and see families sharing in holiday picnics and outdoor activities, I feel a tiny bit of sadness for what I missed out on. I am happy for them, but sad for me. Holidays still make me feel rather dysfunctional. No matter what, I'm grateful for what I have and I can't change the past.

My ground floor corner apartment makes it easy to take my dog, Clinton, in and out. The apartment is extremely tiny, but it is the best place I have ever lived! Finally, the dream I shared with Mern when we were kids, to live on the water, is now my reality. I find it calming and very peaceful; exactly what I need at this point in my life. If I begin to feel sad, I just have to look through my patio doors and my spirits are lifted instantly by Mother Nature. The water helps to center my chi. And, as another sweet life bonus, my boyfriend and I have our own apartments, yet we are close enough to walk over to see each other in one minute. We are in the same complex, but one entryway apart.

Chapter 23

Steven, My Second Chance

In my first interview with a Sierra bear
we were frightened and embarrassed, both of us,
but the bear's behavior was better than mine.
~John Muir~

I had wanted to learn Tai Chi for a very long time. Tai Chi is a form of ancient martial arts, used in self-defense and the promotion of inner peace. I first became aware of the practice when I was at Ohio State. I saw people on campus performing these strange, slow movements and was fascinated. Finally, decades later, I took a class at a senior community center. That particular class was very disappointing. The group spent entirely too much time seated and talking about local gossip in their community. I was relieved when the instructor took a summer hiatus after just a few months. Then a stroke of luck happened. My friend, Randi, told me of a class she had just joined. Randi and I had become very close friends shortly after I met her at Weight Watchers. She was our team leader and I give her one-half the credit for my successful weight loss journey at that time. She is the most positive, nonjudgmental, encouraging, caring person I have ever met. I sincerely appreciate the friendship that has come from that chance meeting six years ago. Meanwhile, I tried out her Tai Chi class and found it to be a perfect fit. I am still enrolled in that class five years later!

The instructor, Nancy, is like our own guru. She is extremely professional, sweet, and humorous. Nancy is organized and dedicated to her students. Her brain works in amazing ways. Not only do I love this Tai Chi class, but the most unexpected thing happened shortly after I joined. I met Steven!

I was not interested in dating anyone and hadn't much since my Bermuda accident. My RSD prevented me from being close to people. Anyhow, one day this guy in the front row turned around and spoke to me. He told me about walking around the grounds where our Tai Chi class was held. River's Edge was a spirituality and wellness community, housed in the nun's convent next to St. Joseph's Academy. It was a beautiful, quaint setting. One campus building sort of resembled Hogwarts, from the *Harry Potter* movies. Unfortunately, since COVID's onset, we are no longer permitted to use that facility because that would put the nuns in a severe health risk situation. We are currently housed elsewhere. One additional bonus of having a class at River's Edge was that Steven and I reconnected with Sister Juanita. She lived in that convent and we saw her quite often.

Steven and I exchanged a few sentences and that was it. I didn't see him back in that class for several weeks. Turns out he had some serious dental work done and needed to heal. I found myself actually thinking about him. I was impressed to see a guy in Tai Chi and felt he must be a good man. There were two other men in the group at the time, but Steven wore cute little red sneakers with cargo shorts and I thought he was a clean-cut kind of guy. I noticed right away what a gentleman he was. He helped people fold up their chairs, held doors open, and was polite to everyone. I knew he was special right away.

The next time Steven came back I was looking out the window at the beautiful autumn colors. He offered to take me to see the grounds right then. I grabbed my friend, Randi, on the way out so she could chaperone this adventure. First thing off, we walked right into an old cemetery. After a brief tour of the grounds, we headed back to our cars. Randi left and

Steven asked if I would like to go to Peace, Love, and Little Donuts for coffee and a donut. I said, "First of all, I don't drink coffee. And secondly, I don't eat donuts." I tend to be very truthful and right to the point, perhaps without always considering the other person's feelings. I realize I was undoubtedly protecting myself from the unknown. I wasn't comfortable that he was asking me out, even for coffee. I think Steven was just shocked and said, "Okay. Maybe another time." Then off he drove. I was somewhat surprised he left so abruptly.

The following week, we talked at length in the sitting area of the convent. We set a date, October 28, 2016, to go out to dinner. We talked nightly on the phone after that conversation. Steven's restaurant choice was Pier W. Once again, I was impressed. Pier W is an upscale restaurant in Cleveland with fabulous seafood, scenic views of Lake Erie's Cleveland skyline, and a live piano player on the weekends. When the day of our first date came around, Steven called and came up with some excuse for changing the location. He thought Pier W was too much for the first date and wondered how he could ever impress me after that. Steven was very nervous about my dietary needs and drove to the restaurant prior to our date. He wanted to make sure everything went well. He had also driven up and down Bagley Road, checking out all the restaurants to see their gluten-free options. Finally, he settled on the Brown Derby.

I met him there and split the check because I didn't want any obligations. That first date went much better than I had expected and I felt very comfortable being with Steven. We conversed nonstop and laughed a great deal. We discussed our early lives and how different our families were. Steven and I talked about our career paths and experiences. The notion of what constitutes a good movie or satisfying music was debated. We discovered very quickly that we do not share a common interest in either of those topics. However, at dinner we decided that we do have similar views on politics and religion. We both had a lot of fun. That restaurant became known as our "Brown W." Exactly one year later, on the anniversary of our first date, we did make it to the real Pier W and were not at all disappointed.

We walked in Lakeview Cemetery and ate at Tommy's on Coventry for our second date. Next, we went to BW to see a great student production of *West Side Story*. Prior to the show, we had dinner at Zach's Steakhouse on Bagley Road. The food and service were both bad, and we have never returned. Despite that, we had front row seats for the show and the production was wonderful. In the parking lot, Steven asked if he could kiss me goodnight. I told him he would have to settle for a hug. I still wasn't prepared to face the fact that I was dating again after more than fifteen years. I didn't know how to deal with my nerve condition.

But it was our next big date where Steven won me over. In December we went to Severance Hall for dinner and a performance. The Cleveland Orchestra and a small chorus accommodated the large screen showing of *It's a Wonderful Life.* Steven had reserved Box Seats! Such an amazing setting, holiday decorations everywhere, fabulous music, and a perfect feel-good movie! He could not have planned a more romantic evening if he tried. I even wore a new black velvet dress and Fergalicious boots! Yep, they were actually called that exact name; designed by Fergie from the Black-eyed Peas. After the performance, we drove downtown to see the beautiful holiday lights on Public Square. It was an absolutely perfect evening. Steven won my heart that night and he got his first kiss!

Currently, the two of us are very happy in our relationship and choose not to marry again. Our independence and living alone are very important to us. I don't know that either Steven or I, could really live with someone, as we are both set in our ways, and have been for a very long time. I have been divorced for nearly 43 years already. Steven and I love each other and are committed in a long-term relationship. We even exchanged beautiful forever rings! We each appreciate our arrangement and enjoy spending time together. Pre-COVID, Steven and I participated in a great deal of activities. During this pandemic time, we have scaled back our social events. Steven and I do enjoy our date nights, at least twice a week. Typically, we stay in and play cards, board games, or watch a movie. But of course, it's usually very difficult to find a movie we can agree upon. I am a *Silence of the Lambs* kind of girl, while Steven is more of a *Princess Bride* type of guy. We see each other, at least briefly, nearly every day. Most of the time we laugh a lot! And naturally, Tai Chi is still a big part of our lives.

Steven is a good guy. I tell him that his mother raised him well. He and his only sibling, David, come from a very good family. He loved his parents dearly and often affectionately quotes them. Their family originally lived in California, but moved to Bay Village, Ohio in 1959. After eleven years the family returned to California. Steven went to college to be a forest ranger but ended up with a long career in food service. He worked as a chef at Lake Tahoe, where he met the woman he ended up marrying. They returned to the Cleveland area and lived in Berea. The largest part of Steven's career was in food service at the Cleveland Clinic. Like me, Steven was married only once, and he has three gorgeous daughters. Although his ex-wife lives less than two blocks away from us, Steven has not seen her one time in the twenty years they have been divorced. I have never met his ex-wife formally, but coincidentally, she did nearly back her car into me as I walked past her driveway one time. The poor woman rolled down her car window and apologized profusely. Maybe it's a good thing she didn't know who I was. As of this month, Steven is the proud Poppy of four beautiful granddaughters.

Steven is kind, sensitive, and a gentleman who treats me like a queen. He still opens my car door, carries things for me, holds my hand, and continually makes sure I am safe. Steven even catches mice for me!

He genuinely loves me and is proud to be in this relationship. When I met Steven, I was at my perfect goal weight. I had just lost 128 pounds through the Weight Watchers program. I had long, permed hair and was thin. That was five years ago. I have had numerous health problems and surgeries since we first met. Steven has taken great care of me whenever help was needed. Meanwhile, I have gained way too much weight back to write the amount here. Also, my long hair was cut. And he still loves me! He is a good man! Steven has since joined Weight Watchers with me where he has achieved and maintained his perfect weight—I'm proud of him. Our absolute favorite thing to do is traveling to Yosemite National Park in California. I was always an ocean person and vacation had to be at a beach. Our license plates are O2OCEAN and OH2YOSE. He introduced me to the notion of mountain views from deep in the valley, giant cascading waterfalls, and the phenomenal Pacific coast. I had been out west, but not as far as California, or the Pacific Ocean. Never could I have imagined the beauty those places hold. We have been to Yosemite four times now and every single time has been unique. We are already booked for our fifth visit there in October 2022.

Steven and I had our share of bad luck on the first Yosemite trip. He broke a tooth from a Good and Plenty candy. I had a severe allergic reaction to sage when I loved the scent and put two little buds in my pocket! Two days later, I fell off the tour tram and hit my head on a concrete curb. We took two ambulances to the Mariposa ER, which was an hour away. Turns out that on our visit to Bodie, the old, abandoned gold rush site, I unknowingly placed a curse on us. I had pocketed a tiny triangular stone because I liked the shape. Later, we learned that according to ghost-hunter lore, anyone who takes anything away from Bodie will be punished. The historic park receives weekly letters from people returning tiny souvenirs so they can lift their curses.

We were extremely grateful to our Tai Chi instructor, Nancy, who went way above and beyond. She met with us on numerous occasions and allowed us to make videos of her demonstrating our favorite exercises. She took the time to prepare us to perform Tai Chi in the most beautiful mountain settings possible. Steven also starred in a Tai Chi video in Lee Vining! That video is pure entertainment and continues to make us laugh without failure. Thanks to Nancy, we regularly make sure we do some Tai Chi in the beautiful park. One day we would love to have Nancy accompany us to Yosemite, where we could all perform Tai Chi together in that amazing setting.

Yosemite never fails to provide exciting adventures. One year, we experienced a rolling electrical blackout for three days. At night, it was so dark outside we couldn't see our hands in front of our faces. We encountered numerous black bears, bobcats, and mule deer; often up close and personal. At Yosemite, we have seen nearly dry waterfalls rapidly changing to thunderous, rushing "bomb cyclone" falls, all in the same week. We have enjoyed the company of Steven's brother, David, and his wife, Kathleen, a couple of times. Once, we stayed in an unheated tent where it was so cold, we could see our breath when we were in bed. Luckily, that was just one night. Normally, we book a suite in the Yosemite Valley Lodge. These are just a few of our adventures. The bottom line is we will continue to visit Yosemite Park whenever we are able, to seek out new experiences. We love it that much.

I met Steven when I was 65 years old. Who knew a person could meet a soulmate at that stage in life without actually looking? And that same person would truly enhance her quality of life? Oh, that's right, Steven claims he knew from the first moment we spoke to one another. It took me a little longer to catch on. Suddenly, once again I had a traveling buddy, someone to laugh with, a theater companion, and a best friend.

I am honestly grateful for all the joy and pleasure he has added to my life. More than five years after our first date, we are still enjoying our relationship. Steven has a very big piece of my heart, and I cannot imagine life without him.

CHAPTER 24

My Health

You can destroy your now by worrying about tomorrow.
~Janis Joplin~

As I write this chapter I have to say, I had a recent medical scare. That incident prompted me to complete all my paperwork for a Last Will and Testament, a Living Will, a list of all accounts with passwords and, Power of Attorney for Finances and Health Care. I thank my kids for agreeing to take on those last two responsibilities: Lyndie Health Care, and G.J. Finances. I also arranged with Case Western Reserve University to donate my whole body to their medical school upon my death. It is important that I assist in furthering the knowledge of others, even when I am dead. In addition, I have always desired to put my life story into written words. Now, I suddenly feel an urgency to do so. I want my kids to know my story and they know so little about my background. Hence, this book.

The incentive for this urgency is a breathing condition. For nearly six months now, I have been fighting a severe breathing issue. It felt like I could only get air from my mouth and the very top of my throat. After two prior unsuccessful trips to the Express Care, on March 9, 2022, I went to see my primary care physician, Dr. Lucy O'Brien. I could not breathe. My blood pressure was 184/108 and my pulse ox was 84. My blood pressure was usually right around 120/79 or so. A normal pulse ox range is 95–100. She didn't mess around. A siren blaring ambulance took me from her office to Southwest Hospital where they admitted me. After more x-rays, bloodwork, oxygen, nebulizer, heart monitor, EKG, cardiogram, therapy, and a brain scan due to a severe headache, finally a CT scan found double pneumonia in the lungs.

I felt better in the hospital those four days, but things were about the same when I returned home. Two minutes walking, talking too much, or climbing just four steps, all resulted in the inability to catch my breath. It is a horrible, scary feeling! I followed up with my doc, who tends to be quite thorough. She prescribed more antibiotics, steroids, powder inhaler twice daily, blood pressure meds, short-acting inhaler, and continued the nebulizer. The doctor ordered a complete blood workup, including a thyroid test. All were normal or negative, but a breathing test had abnormal results. I also completed a sleep study and will wear a CPAP for sleep apnea. Currently, I am seeing a pulmonary specialist who says my lungs will take a long while to recover, due to the amount of scarring from the double pneumonia.

I am still experiencing shortness of breath with the slightest exertion, but I do see minor improvement. Breathing problems can be so serious. And now, as of June 9, 2022, I can add COVID to my list of illnesses. My three vaccinations seemed to have helped to keep my case mild. Only a cough and the lingering breathing difficulty remain.

I chose to write this particular chapter, and all the details on health, so that my kids could be made aware of my medical issues, which can often be hereditary. I have almost no medical history from my own dysfunctional family, and that can be a deficit when trying to diagnose my ailments. My wish is that I do not pass anything on that will cause my kids pain. Unfortunately, I believe Lyndie has already inherited my arthritis problems. I do think it's important to note that many of my family members died rather young. My mother, father, two half-sisters, and my younger brother, all died in their sixties.

So right here, right now, I would be remiss should I choose to ignore the degree of mental illness in my family. Again, because I lack a complete family medical history, I shall approach the topic in a piecemeal manner. I will do my best to relate what I know or what siblings have told me.

My father, Frank Sr., clearly had a mental disorder. The Diagnostic and Statistical Manual of Mental Disorders (DSM-5) clearly includes the pedophilic disorder, as well as an alcohol use disorder. My father was definitely an alcoholic and a pedophile. He had cirrhosis of the liver caused by excessive drinking, and emphysema from smoking. I remember how his fingers were stained with nicotine from constantly holding his cigarettes. Frank Sr. was seriously overweight and I recall how he often tried to drop pounds by starving himself, eating only one steak with a Diet Rite Cola every day. Shortly before he died, in his early sixties, he was diagnosed with acute respiratory failure, congested heart failure, and chronic obstructive lung disease. That's just freaky because it's too close to my own current personal health problems.

The mental health issues seem to be even more pronounced on my mother's side of the family, starting with her. May had issues with alcohol, depression, and a nervous breakdown. I know she received shock therapy at some point. Her reactions were always a bit off. For example, when I told May that Jim Wyman was divorcing me and had found someone else, her reaction was, "Oh, poor Jimmy!" I didn't dare question that one. She seemed to laugh at the strangest things and often stared off into space. May showed little emotion, certainly not love. Sometimes I wondered if she had a lobotomy. My mother died from peritonitis due to her diabetic complications.

Schizophrenia was a terrible enemy within our family. My brother, Frank Jr., was formally diagnosed with paranoid schizophrenia. He heard voices and hallucinated. Frank was extremely intelligent but became obviously ill as a late teen during his first year at college. He then spent the rest of his days on various medications and was institutionalized until he died. Once my brother was diagnosed, he never experienced another normal day of living. Frank hated his life and attempted suicide on multiple occasions. The only time I saw my adult brother happy was in his last few years. About twice a month, when I visited him, we were allowed to go out and we'd take a short drive to see Lake Erie. He never got out of the car, but just stared at the waves so contentedly. The joy only lasted about five minutes before he'd say, "I'm ready. Take me home." Frank loved the water just as much as my sister and I did. My poor brother lived with those terrible inner demons from his disorder for more than forty years, until he ultimately died from heart failure in his early sixties.

Bruce Coleman, my half-brother (same mother), also suffered from paranoid schizophrenia. I believe he was able to function on his own while taking medications. He struggled a great deal in his relationships. Bruce was a smart guy. He was a civil engineer who was involved in designing several highway and flood control projects in the Columbus and Cleveland areas. At age 81, Bruce died in 2021, from diabetes and coronary disease.

His brother, Howard Coleman, is alive and well. Also, a very smart guy, Howard, was a councilman at one time in Ohio. Howard is a kind, articulate man who is easy to talk to. I appreciate his acute sense of humor. Unfortunately, I do not know him very well.

Gail Coleman Thompson, my half-sister (also the same mother), suffered from several mental issues. I don't know her formal diagnosis. Gail was another bright sibling. She graduated from nursing school and ended up married and living in Alaska. I was told that she had some sort of breakdown during her brief one-year marriage. Gail left Alaska and moved to California, where she lived for most of her life. When our mother died, Gail began to call and write to me. Unfortunately, Gail had chronic health issues, was diabetic, had breast cancer, and weighed about 400 pounds. She was in a motorized wheelchair until she was bedridden. The time came when Gail's caregiver said in-home care would no longer be possible due to her size. Gail was told she had to go into a nursing home. She chose not to do so and found a permanent solution. Gail committed suicide in her sixties.

Her full sister, (again the same mother), Barbara Coleman, was in college at Bowling Green in Ohio, before moving to California. I did not see Barbara, or Gail, very often after we left the foster home in 1959. I believe I saw them only once or twice after that. Somehow, we got together when Gail graduated from nursing school. We had not been in touch for many years but reconnected, through phone calls and letters, when our mother died in the mid-1980s. I finally had a chance to see Barbara when she came to Cleveland for a visit, in August 2013. Upon returning to California, Barbara began writing to me more often, so we could get to know each other. Sadly, my sister, Barbara, died from sepsis, following a surgical procedure, just seven months after her Cleveland visit. Too young, too soon, she was gone on March 28, 2012. Barbara has two sons and would be happy to know that I met both of them in the past few years. Her youngest, Nathan, came to Cleveland and stopped by so I could meet him. He admittingly has some issues with authority and seems to choose a difficult, troubled life. I hardly know him.

I also had the opportunity to meet Barbara's oldest son, Eddy, and his gorgeous wife, Cheryl. They live atop a mountain with a breath-taking view in Santa Cruz, California. Their relationship is beautiful, and they are totally in love. Cheryl and Eddy's lives are full of gourmet meals, creativity, art, and beautiful craftsmanship. They are both extremely talented people. Fittingly, the dog, Wrenny, is a frisbee catching award-winning champion. Steven and I had an opportunity to meet Eddy and Cheryl and to spend a little time becoming acquainted as guests in their lovely home. Both are amazing people and very supportive of one another.

My full sister, Fran, goes through her daily life surviving on her own. She met her college sweetheart, Derek Mitchell, at Case Western Reserve University. Derek was from Bermuda. They were married and lived in Toronto, and then Bermuda, more than 25 years, but have since divorced. Fran and Derek have a beautiful, brilliant daughter, Kirsten, who lives in London. Fran really loves her daughter but doesn't get to see her very often. I don't know if my sister has ever been formally diagnosed with any obvious issues like depression, or social anxieties. Though we grew up together and experienced some of the same traumatic events and conditions, we rarely discussed them. I think Fran is more of an introvert than I am. She does not like any type of confrontation or discourse. On the other hand, I am a fighter. Fran's a rather private person and I always found our relationship very awkward. It was difficult to really know her, even when we lived together.

As for me, I realize there is a very fine line we all walk between wellness and having mental disorders. I could probably make some therapist very wealthy with my own issues. For example, I choose to eat too much when dealing with my stuff. That could be seen as a mental health issue. Also, I have so much pain in my body I have to deliberately choose not to depress nearly every single day. I choose to be happy, though it's not always easy. But I think I'm okay.

There is no doubt that for the most part, I have not taken good care of this vessel of life, my body. I have been overweight at least 80% of my lifetime. There have been moments when I have been at the "correct" weight, but that is only through determination and great effort. Unfortunately, I fall back to old habits only too easily. I like to eat for any reason. I eat under stress. I eat when I relax. I eat to celebrate, and I eat to forget. I have just never learned to value myself more than I value food. Although I eat "healthier foods" than you might think, the problem is I eat way too much of them—constantly! Oh, I do have my chocolate, chips, and cheese addictions also. I realize my weight seriously contributes to my health problems.

Most of my health troubles relate to either my gut, my bones, or chronic severe pain matters. I have had way too many surgeries, as far as I am concerned. On that extensive list is repeated hernia repair, and it needs to be done again. The last hernia surgery was unsuccessful because they had to take out my appendix and part of my colon due to scar tissue complications. That was ugly and caused an internal abdominal infection for nearly four months. I don't want to go through that again.

Also related to the gut is my celiac disease. I wasn't diagnosed until 2005 or so. I probably had it all my life, but doctors just attributed my digestive problems to "irritable bowel syndrome" and stress. Misdiagnoses can happen! Funny, when I was unknowingly pregnant with G.J., the doctor inaccurately diagnosed him as the flu. Anyhow, celiac means I cannot tolerate any amount of gluten in my body. I tend to get abdominal pains, diarrhea, and sometimes throw up immediately if I eat any gluten. My undiagnosed celiac led to malnourishment and eventually osteoporosis, or brittle bone disease.

The moped accident in Bermuda shattered my bones into numerous pieces. Most likely, I already had osteoporosis but was unaware until my bone density scan clearly revealed it. I have had two trimalleolar (three bone) ankle breaks, three Jones fracture foot breaks, a multiple fractured humerus, several broken toes, and a broken nose. Unfortunately, most of those broken bones resulted in chronic osteoarthritis. In addition, I have scoliosis, or curvature of the spine, which causes stabbing pain in my back and neck. Arthritis is everywhere. In 2020 I had to have thumb surgery on my right hand. The pain became so unbearable that I could only hold my nearly unusable hand and cry. It's better now, but that darn arthritis found its way into other parts of the same hand and my wrist.

As I stated earlier, I experience a great deal of pain in this body. That sad reality hit me hard one day when Lyndie told me that she has never known me at a time when I did not have pain. I had never realized it before, but that was certainly true. My first trimalleolar ankle break was when she was under three years old. I believe my RSD began at that time. That ankle never seemed to recover. I have had blood clots twice, one traveled to my lung. I also experienced a grapefruit-sized hematoma in my abdomen, right after my gall bladder surgery. My ankle was always severely swollen, discolored, sensitive to touch, warm, inflexible, and finally arthritic. I have walked with a limp since that fall down the school steps in 1979. As of that fall, I also have to wear compression stockings full-time.

Of course, the most notable problem related to bones is likely my shoulder. The nerve damage and total shoulder replacement resulted in very limited use of that left arm. Consequently, in Tai Chi class, I am able to use only one arm. I can lift the left arm about 35 degrees, where a normal range of motion is 180 degrees. Luckily, I get some use out of the arm because I can bend the elbow. The left hand has limited ability and gets very stiff. I am unable to make a closed fist, so I drop a lot of things. The hand is pretty sensitive to different textures and temperatures. However, there has been improvement over the years. When I was first diagnosed with RSD, I could close my eyes and touch my right finger with my RSD left fingers to accurately describe the exact shape of the prints on my right finger. That's how sensitive the left hand was! Still, it is not at all unusual for my fingertips to turn purple when I am stressed or cold. Sudden and loud noises, or movements, still scare the crap out of me. All that is just part of the RSD. I have learned to cope with it and to avoid or adapt my own behaviors in order to succeed.

My body is my body alone. I have made all my own choices regarding this body. Any female surgeries I've had were spread out over many years. I have had a few. Among them was a tubal ligation, and after some time, I needed a hysterectomy because of heavy bleeding and clotting. Prior to the tubal ligation, I had more than one abortion. I was unable to take oral contraceptives, after a pulmonary embolism. I tried an IUD but had complications with it slipping and causing an infection. So, yes, I chose abortion. I am only telling this because I do not wish to pretend to be someone other than exactly who I am. I am a strong advocate for women's rights to make their own decisions about their own bodies. I don't judge others in that respect, and I don't expect to be judged for my personal beliefs. This is a scary time for women, as we see our rights being stripped away. I am afraid the fictional television series, *The Handmaid's Tale*, hits too close to home.

I asked not to be judged, but I must admit, it is sometimes very difficult for me to understand the values, beliefs, and actions of others. I get that people want to hang on to their own beliefs, no matter the cost. Unfortunately, we have seen how that plays out during this horrible COVID Pandemic. In just two years, we have already lost over one million people in the United States. The political controversy over masks and vaccines is outrageous. Hospitals are bulging at the seams and medical personnel are dropping out at an extremely high rate. They are burned out. It's been nonstop for more than two years and they are just exhausted.

I realize that everyone wants to return to their old lives. Too many have lost their homes, jobs, friends, and loved ones to COVID. Patience is short. People have had enough and want it to be over. I get that. Never the less, people refused to wear simple masks in public places, way back when the pandemic first started to spread in this country. Often, those same folks refused to get the vaccination shots. They have rights! No one can tell them what to do! Too many individuals get their information from the internet or other ill-informed sources. They refuse to listen to science.

My friend Mern was one of them. So was her sister, Margaret. They were misinformed from the very beginning and refused to listen to reason. I lost my dear friend because she was so stubborn. I repeatedly tried to convince Mern to be vaccinated, or at least wear a mask out in public. She refused. She spent five weekends at my apartment last summer. We argued, watched fireworks, ate Chinese, listened to live concerts across Coe Lake, and played rummy all hours of the night. Mostly, like old times, we just laughed and laughed. I didn't know that she would be dead just 13 days after I last saw her. Our 61-year-old friendship ended abruptly. Mern died from COVID on October 3, 2022, and her sister, Margaret, died just two weeks later. I am still mad at my friend.

CHAPTER 25

My Poetry

Poetry is nearer to vital truth than history.
~Plato~

Poetry was an important part of my life. Writing my own poetry was a way I could let my feelings out, sans judgment. This life story would not be complete without a few of my favorite entries. The reader has an opportunity to learn a great deal about me through my poetry.

WHEN I WRITE POEMS

I can write poems that will make you cry—
Poems that will leave not one dry eye.
I could write poems that can sing the blues.
My damaged heart is not recent news.

My poems could be collected for a bestselling book.
People would read them and have that look.
That look of agreement knowing what it's like—
To struggle through relationships that cause such strife.

My collection of poems could touch people's hearts.
They wouldn't put them down once they start.
The poems I write would help others see—
It's not so easy to set yourself free.

My poems could explain how we protect our hearts—
How we plan our actions right from the start.
My poems could allow you to see yourself in me—
Those poems may even help to set you free.

~Patty Wyman~
June 7, 1985

This was a poem for my daughter, Lyndie. When she was a freshman, we had just dropped her off at college. I knew she would be successful no matter what she chose to do. But it was still hard to see her so grown-up and completely ready to be on her own. I am so proud of who Lyndie is and all that she has become. To this day she still believes in equality for all and continues to fight for the rights of others. Lyndie is one of the best human beings I know.

IT'S TIME TO LET GO: POEM FOR MY DAUGHTER

For some strange reason, this poem has been my most difficult to write.
It's not that I haven't tried, both day and night.
I didn't understand, but now I know—
The writer's block was caused by not letting go.

So, you're eighteen and they call you an adult.
The title doesn't fit when my thoughts come out.
To me, you're the first baby whom I gave birth.
You'll always be my baby, while I'm on Earth.

I've watched you crawl and then walk.
I was there when you learned to talk.
You went off to school once before.
At that time, you were only four.

You've gone through stages with friend and foe.
There will be more stages, that much I know.
You had a fear of trying new things.
Then suddenly you were on stage all ready to sing.

You developed your character as time went by.
Sometimes I watched from a distance and let myself cry.
You are hardworking, loyal, and honest I know.
You believe in equality for all, not just for show.

For someone you love, you'll go above and beyond.
Holding your thoughts is something you work on.
Athletic ability is also a part of you.
Competing is something you naturally do.

My dear daughter, to me you're a rainbow full of multiple hues.
You are exactly the daughter I'd deliberately choose.
Keep those expectations high of yourself and others.
Don't settle for less, even from your mother.

The future is yours, grab it with all of your might.
When times are tough be ready to fight.
Be true to yourself, yet sensitive to others.
Remember this advice and love from your mother.

I love you more than you could possibly know.
There! Now I guess I'm ready to let go.

I love you Lyndie, Mommy
~Patty Wyman~
August 1994

G.J. was the quarterback at Cuyahoga Heights High School. I wrote this poem after a spectacular football season in 1994. It was the school's first winning season since 1986 and they were undefeated going into their final game. There was a big controversy when the school principal was ultimately fired after celebrating in the end zone before the clock ran out. In the last few seconds of the game a tying touchdown was thrown. It doesn't get much more exciting than that! The principal ran and jumped onto a pile of his players in the end zone. Cuyahoga Heights received a penalty for the principal's actions, eventually resulting in a missed extra point. They lost the game in overtime. It was big news across the country. Jay Leno surprisingly joked about it on the *Tonight Show*. The gossip magazine, the *National Enquirer* repeatedly tried to interview G.J., but he ignored them, just as he did with all other questions or comments. I was, and still am, proud of G. for so many reasons.

I don't think I ever gave him a copy of this poem. I felt like it wasn't finished and likely forgot about it. Hope he can enjoy it all these years later.

DEAR MR. QUARTERBACK: POEM FOR MY SON

I have watched you from the stands and screamed out your name.
Your intelligent, skillful plays have bought you fame.
Your quarterback fake was a bit hard to see,
But your greatest fan was actually me.

I watched you call plays and powerfully lead your team.
I noticed your kindness; you could never be mean.
You never gave up when times were tough.
Your strength and will were always enough.

You quickly forgave the mistakes of others.
Took on your teammates as though they were brothers.

You were a real team player, never taking all credit.
When gossip came out, you never even read it.

You never chose to point a finger of blame.
Your actions were never a cause for shame.
For this football season you can be so proud.
I've said it before, but I'll say it aloud.
I love you with all my heart—
As I have from the very start.

It's who you are that makes you great.
Being an awesome quarterback was just your fate.
Your personality is what makes you a star.
Be true to yourself and you'll always go far.

I love you G.J., Mommy
~Patty Wyman~
Fall 1994

The next poem describes the feelings I had about my mother. Less than a year before she died, May lost her leg to diabetes. I repaid her kindness for letting me stay with her earlier. She lived in my living room for about ten months, and I still had no emotional connection to her. When my mother died, I did not feel genuine sorrow. Rather, I felt a little sadness for what never was. And perhaps I actually felt a sense of relief. This is a poem I wrote and read for her memorial service.

ODE TO MY MOTHER

Dear Mother? Mom? Mommy? Ma?
It's so difficult to say those words.
They're all sounds from me you have never heard.
Circumstances—just the way it was,
Made me so unsure of love.

You gave me birth, so I've been told.
How is it I let you grow old?
I kept from you my soul and heart.
Guess I've protected myself right from the start.

Our lives were separate for the longest time.
Got out of that foster home when I was nine.
You couldn't visit; I remember that.
But to you I should tip my hat.

Your life was hard; of that, I'm sure.
You were strong and tough, and pretty secure.
Working hard carrying trays—
In those restaurants nights and days.

I never thought I knew you well,
Until last Christmastime when you went through hell.
It was only then I saw your strength and will.
Your medical struggle was all uphill.

I attempted to find my stems and roots.
It wasn't easy walking in my boots.
The unknown was scary—so much untold.
Would my earlier life ever unfold?

I don't think you ever heard me mention love.
That was a subject I handled with kid gloves.
It wasn't you I didn't like—
It was the struggle in life that was such a strife.

You were gentle and kind; not a mean bone in you.
You were independent and a real survivor, too.
For you I'm sorry that life was so rough.
But it's you I thank for making me tough.

You see—life was painful, but I learned a lot.
And now I know how to survive with all that I've got.
Thank you for that!

~Patty Wyman~
November 1985

I was thirty-four years old, divorced, mother of two little ones, nearly finished with my master's degree, teaching, and just really worn out. This poem was written on a spring break in Bermuda.

THE STORM BREWING IN ME

The clouds were heavy, dark, and grey—
Hiding the sun that brightens my day.
I must confess—
My head is a mess!

The water's hue—
that special blue.
I'm full of emotion—
With no real devotion.

Not a longtail in sight—
This day or night.
Why am I confused—
And feel all used?

The tide's rolling in—
Right around that bend.
I just want to stop and unwind.
Someone please, unravel the twine.

The warm breeze of the beautiful ocean—
Bending the tall cedar trees in motion.
My life's a mess—out of control.
I want to please, let it all go.

Bermuda, Bermuda! You're just the same.
Yet somehow your weather is playing a game.
There's a real storm inside of me.
Feels like lightning striking a tree.

More rain than they've seen in twenty years,
Could bring many tourists to tears.
I'm okay with all the rain——
That's not the source of my own pain.

The cruise ship sits in the distance so silent.
Weathering a storm can be quite violent.
The real storm is inside of me.
How crazed can my life really be?

The island's weather is sure to clear.
The colorful rainbow is so very near.
What about me? Will my problems go?
There is a clearing, I guess I know.

~Patty Wyman~
April 10, 1985

I wrote several poems about love. None of them were pretty. Wow! I am just realizing that I was in a dark place for a very long time. I am grateful that I am no longer there. Finally, I can allow myself to love and be loved. This poem was written nearly eight years after my divorce.

BAD LOVE

This is the poem I have waited to write.
Somehow, I've chosen to continue my flight.
"Play the victim" it's been called.
When love is mentioned, I am appalled.

It hurt so bad—it won't let me rest.
No other relationship will get my best.
Why do I choose to feel sorry for me?
Why can't I fly and set myself free?

Do I stay stuck because it is safe?
Why don't I move to another place?
Let my heart go—let it feel?
Is pain the only emotion that's real?

I don't want to love—I do want out.
Sometimes I cry or scream and shout.
Love sucks! I'll never believe in it again.
You can save it for your own friends.

For me, love has never been true.
Don't take it away because you don't know what else to do.
Divorced parents, foster home, abusive father, and such.
My ex-husband taking away love was too much.

They're all lies—they're not real.
Was it I who asked for such a rotten deal?
Sounds pessimistic of me, but I know I'm not.
Just wondering about all the bad love I got.

Somehow, I have to wonder if it's me.
Do you think anyone loved me before I was three?

~Patty Wyman~
June 6, 1985

CHAPTER 26

Conclusion

To know that we know what we know,
and to know that we do not know what we do not know,
that is true knowledge.
~Nicholas Copernicus~

This last poetry entry was recently written upon near completion of this book. Self-reflection of all previous chapters made me realize the purpose in my book had changed somewhere during the writing process. I went from writing to inform, to also writing to inspire. Looking back at one's life can be a cathartic experience if allowed. It is interesting to compare my poetry from nearly 40 years ago to now. I have finally reached a mature stage of giving myself permission to be happy and loved. I am worth it!

MY MESSAGE TO YOU

The person I am, came through a difficult past.
Learning life's hard lessons was never fast.
I've come so far and have personally grown.
That doesn't mean you never heard me moan.

From early on, my life was tough.
Leaving my emotional edges rather rough.
Love was forbidden from my protected heart.
I realized that quickly, right from the start.

My family was broken, and so out of sync.
Close friends of mine provided the link.
The link to survival and being happy.
Helped me forget my life was so crappy.

Emotional bonds were tight with my pets—
When counting on humans was often off bets.
What I want you to consider and really know,
Is that my life choices put me in full control.

I could have cried and crawled into a hole.
But I never wanted to quit or forfeit my soul.
My soul had pure fight and believed in me.
Though I had little love before I was three.

Somehow, I wanted to be happy and believed that I could.
Now I see clearly that I truly understood.
I knew that my happiness would come from only me.
No other human could set me free.

My true freedom came with a price.
Some of my relationships weren't so nice.
Through self-reflection, I think I've progressed.
This time my heart's protectors are at rest.

Now I am free to love without doubt.
No need to leave, to scream, or shout.
I know now that I am worthy and that's hard to say.
For a very long time that area was grey.

Could I be worthy, the way my family treated me?
The problem was theirs, not mine, I now can see.
I have value far beyond what you know.
I can inspire others and help them grow.

My inspiration has both substance and depth.
I can give others hope with each and every breath.
I've come so far by taking the reins.
If you do just that, you'll see the gains.

No more excuses; just take control.
Live your life and set a worthy goal.
Don't allow others to control who you are.
Make it happen; don't just wish upon a star.
Your goal should drive you in every way.
Never lose sight of it, night or day.

For you, I wish happiness, but I can't hand it to you.
You're the one to make that happen by all that you do.
Take in this poem and heed my words.
Then go live your life and make your heart heard.

~Patty Wyman~
June 15, 2022

There is nothing to writing.
All you do is sit down to a typewriter and bleed.
~Ernest Hemingway~

I have bled profusely and honestly in this book. Now you know the rest of my story. It's time to go out and live your own great story and then write about it.

~THE END~

CPSIA information can be obtained
at www.ICGtesting.com
Printed in the USA
BVHW051544230523
664715BV00015B/941